EXPERIENCING GOD'S PROVISION

RON FREDRIKS

WESTBOW
PRESS®
A DIVISION OF THOMAS NELSON
& ZONDERVAN

WestBow Press books may be ordered through booksellers or by contacting:

WestBow Press
A Division of Thomas Nelson & Zondervan
1663 Liberty Drive
Bloomington, IN 47403
www.westbowpress.com
844-714-3454

Unless marked otherwise, all scripture quotations are taken
from the New King James Version®. Copyright © 1982 by
Thomas Nelson. Used by permission. All rights reserved.

Scripture quotations marked KJV are taken from the King James Version.

ISBN: 978-1-6642-5849-5 (sc)
ISBN: 978-1-6642-5848-8 (e)

Print information available on the last page.

WestBow Press rev. date: 03/09/2022

CONTENTS

CONTENTS

ACKNOWLEDGMENTS

I am indebted to authors of the past—to Jessie Penn-Lewis, A. W. Pink, Frederick Douglass, Charles Spurgeon, John Newton, Nicholas Herman, J. C. Ryle, and Jonathan Edwards—for their inspired writings and for their insight into the ways of God.

INTRODUCTION

Many think they are safe under the Christian umbrella but just by believing that to be true does not necessarily make it true. Scripture and history are used in this book to bring to light some false premises as well as the fundamentals of salvation and the glorious and victorious life that follows. The challenge for the reader is to prove what is truth and what is false and then "to make your call and election sure" (2 Peter 1:10).

> Not everyone who says to Me, "Lord, Lord," shall enter the kingdom of heaven, but he who does the will of My Father in heaven. Many will say to Me in that day, "Lord, Lord, have we not prophesied in Your name, cast out demons in Your name, and done many wonders in Your name?" And then I will declare to them, "I never knew you; depart from Me, you who practice lawlessness!" (Matthew 7:21-23)

To help us be more cautious about our own possible failure to understand this most important issue, we are told, "Examine yourselves as to whether you are in the faith. Test yourselves. Do you not know yourselves, that Jesus Christ is in you?—unless indeed you are disqualified" (2 Corinthians 13:5). Great Bible scholars such as those Pharisee teachers during Jesus's time missed what God had for them. And for anyone who thinks they're right with God, nothing could be worse than to hear the Lord say, "I never knew you" as seen in Matthew 7:21-23.

Redemption does not necessarily come about by just saying the words given to us in the Bible to say. Redemption and deliverance come about by a proper understanding of what the Bible says, confessing our sins and totally surrendering our life to Him. Unless this is grasped many will have a misunderstanding of what God requires for a true conversion experience. This can be seen in a parable Jesus told, about five out of ten virgins who missed their opportunity to be brought into the wedding chamber:

> Then the kingdom of heaven shall be likened to ten virgins who took their lamps and went out to meet the bridegroom. Now five of them were wise, and five were foolish. Those who were foolish took their lamps and took no oil with them, but the wise took oil in their vessels with their lamps. (Matthew 25:1-4)

When the bridegroom finally arrived at midnight, the virgins who had no oil to light their lamps thought they were ready to meet their master, but were not. Only the prepared ones "went in with him to the wedding; and the door was shut" (Matthew 25:10). When the five virgins later returned with oil, they cried out, "Lord, Lord, open to us!"—but he answered, "Assuredly, I say to you, I do not know you" (Matthew 25:11-12).

The correlation for us today is that many may appear to be Christians, but like those five foolish virgins holding their lamps, they have no oil or substance in their lives to enter the wedding chamber. In the end, they'll hear those tragic words of the Lord: "I do not know you."

It doesn't matter what kind of despicable characters we are, or what wrongs we've done in this life. What does matter is that we're seeking God with an open heart, accepting His way of salvation, and surrendering our will to do whatever is necessary "to be conformed to the image of His Son" (Romans 8:29).

Think of how many throughout history were disillusioned by what they thought Christianity was. Some may realize only when it's too late that they had a dysfunctional relationship with God. But it's not only unbelievers who miss their opportunity of knowing God; many who believe in Christ may also have missed what He has to offer. A professed Christian can get into a life-pattern of thinking his standing and walk before God is fine, and yet find in the end that he has pursued a life with no lasting value.

Scripture tells us, "Be not deceived; God is not mocked: for whatever a man sows, that he will also reap. For he who sows to his flesh will of the flesh reap corruption; but he who sows to the Spirit will of the Spirit reap life everlasting" (Galatians 6:7-8). We're responsible for our actions before God, and thus we're commanded to not be deceived. If we are deceived, God will not be drawn into our folly or be mocked by what we do. We can even be deceived in thinking God has delivered us when that may not be true. Following such a deceptive path is a "sowing to the flesh," which could result in a loss of fellowship with God—or even more catastrophic, eternal separation from God, which is another way of describing Hell.

God knows us completely. He calls us to learn of Him and understand the path He has for us to follow. Jesus says, "Learn from Me, for I am gentle and lowly in heart, and you will find rest for your souls" (Matthew 11:29). Therefore we're told, "Be even more diligent to make your call and election sure, for if you do these things you will never stumble; for so an entrance will be supplied to you abundantly into the everlasting kingdom of our Lord and Savior Jesus Christ" (2 Peter 1:10-11).

When we become transformed by the Spirit of God, we become part of God's family, and He gives us eyes to see and ears to hear. He gives us wisdom, understanding, power, and strength to deal with our old life and to come into His new life. God will speak to us through our mind, conscience, and spirit to make us, by His grace, what He wants us to be: "conformed into the image of His Son" (Romans 8:29). Some things may be offensive to our ego but nothing should hold us back from learning to walk the path He has for us to follow. Being saved by the blood of Christ is not the end of our quest of knowing God, but just the beginning of an eternal and glorious future.

Around 440 a.d., Aurelius Augustinus—better known to us today as Augustine—penned the following words: "Thou hast made us for thyself, O Lord, and our heart is restless until it finds its rest in thee." Until we come to an end of ourselves and pursue the life we're meant to live by His grace, we won't find satisfaction in our souls. An intimately personal relationship with God is His pleasure for us. Don't let anyone persuade you to believe otherwise.

CHAPTER 1

GOD'S PROVISION

Human religion deals mainly with intellectual philosophies, moral principles, and acts of kindness where the main point of Christianity is a change within. Christ substituting Himself in our place as sinners is His act that erases God's charge against us and opens the door for God's Spirit to dwell in us. Our lives are desolate and without meaning until this happens. Through Christ and His Spirit, we become joint heirs with God: "The Spirit Himself bears witness with our spirit that we are children of God, and if children, then heirs—heirs of God and joint heirs with Christ" (Romans 8:16-17). An heir of Christ experiences His life, His peace, His joy, His faith, and more.

Our worship of God should be with a changed heart and should no longer be controlled by a self-heart. The Pharisees, the Jewish religious leaders during Jesus's time, worshiped God with a self-heart, and Jesus questioned them on several occasions and called out their hypocrisy. Although their outward life looked pure and righteous, inwardly they were full of sin.

Nicodemus—a Pharisee and ruler of the Jews—came to Jesus by night to speak with Him. Jesus came right to the point, and told him, "Unless one is born again, he cannot see the kingdom of God" (John 3:3). Only those who've been born anew can see the kingdom of God and think pure and holy thoughts, because they now have His pure and holy nature within them. Christ died "that the body of sin might be done away with, that we should no longer be slaves to sin" (Romans 6:6). In this world we'll never reach perfection, because we never rid ourselves of our fleshly nature, but we can keep it in check with what God has provided.

An intellectual pursuit of God gives one an understanding of who God is and an understanding of what He's trying to achieve, but we won't have true understanding and satisfaction until we experience His life in us. We cannot command God to give this to us as something we're entitled to; instead Jesus tells us, "Seek, and you will find" (Matthew 7:7), and also, "You did not choose Me, but I (God) chose you" (John 15:16). Both statements are true, and we need to be diligent in our search to determine how they work together. Our part is to seek Him, but He needs to draw us unto Him. He needs to draw us into the story. For our unholy self to come to the holy and pure God requires a miracle of grace.

Why should God even want to come into a life so opposite of Him? As Habakkuk said to God, "You are of purer eyes than to behold evil, and cannot look on wickedness" (Habakkuk 1:13), and the apostle John tells us, "In Him is no darkness at all" (1 John 1:5). No matter how much we want to come to Him, it's impossible unless He allows us to see the means He has made available.

This is why we see so many wrong ways of worshiping; each is simply another way that man supposes God should be worshiped. "But now after you have known God, or rather are known by God..." (Galatians 4:9)—those words from the apostle Paul show how God takes the initiative to find and love us. "We love Him because He first loved us" (1 John 4:19)—this is the only reason we can truly love Him. We need this mindset in our pursuit of God, so that we don't think of ourselves too highly by supposing we're desirable to Him because we've cleaned up our life somewhat, or have done a few good deeds.

When it comes to God taking the initiative, listen to what He told the prophet Jeremiah in the Old Testament: "Before I formed you in the womb I knew you; before you were born I sanctified you; I ordained you a prophet to the nations" (Jeremiah 1:45). Then we see Jesus saying, "I am the good shepherd; and I know My sheep, and am known by My own" (John 10:14). Why do we know Him? We know Him because God put it in our heart to know Him. It's all grace. Jesus explains it again when He prays to His Father, "These have known that You sent Me. And I have declared

2

to them Your name, and will declare it, that the love with which You loved Me may be in them, and I in them" (John 17:25-26).

In spite of ourselves—and for some unknown reason—God has mercy on us, reveals Himself to us, and wants to come into our life and be our friend. God desires every person to come to repentance, for He is "longsuffering toward us, not willing that any should perish but that all should come to repentance" (2 Peter 3:9). The Lord is longsuffering and patiently enduring, but the reality is that many will not come to Him, and are on the road to doom and destruction. An example of this is seen when Jesus was talking to the Pharisees, those highly respected religious leaders of His time. He said to them, "You are of your father the devil, and the desires of your father you want to do. He was a murderer from the beginning, and does not stand in the truth, because there is no truth in Him" (John 8:44).

Perhaps you know Jesus's parable about the sower and the seeds in Matthew 13. Some seeds fell by the wayside; some were devoured by the birds; some fell on rocky ground and sprouted there, but later were scorched in the sun; others were choked by thorns. But then there are those that fell on good ground—representing the man or woman "who hears the word and understands it, who indeed bears fruit and produces" (Matthew 13:23). These are the people God speaks to, and to whom Jesus says, "It has been given to you to know the mysteries of the kingdom of heaven" (Matthew 13:11). These are the ones drawn into the story.

We all share in the quality ascribed to Reuben by his father Jacob: "unstable as water" (Genesis 49:4). Our only hope for stability in our deplorable condition lies in the One whom God sent to stand in our place. This One—Jesus—made His righteousness *our* righteousness, and His standing before God as ours, and His life as ours. There's no condition or responsibility on our part to receive this, other than to accept what He has given. Jesus, the second person of the Trinity, lowered Himself to come to this earth: "Though He was rich, yet for your sakes He became poor, that you through His poverty might become rich" (2 Corinthians 8:9).

"In Him [Jesus] was life, and the life was the light of men" (John 1:4). We've all been given a physical life, "for in Him we live and move and have our being" (Acts 17:28). But as you know, the body gets old, decays, and eventually dies. So what's really important is to experience the spiritual life which goes on for eternity. Christ gives us light and life so we can experience what He has to offer and be able to have a relationship with God the Father here, now, and for eternity.

The opposite of God's grace is His wrath. Knowing the consequences of God's wrath should drive us to diligently seek His grace. Christ crucified was a stumbling block to the Jews, and to the Greeks it was foolishness (1 Corinthians 1:23). Accepting what God has to offer through His Son grates against our self-sufficiency and pride, which are part of our sinful nature. But proving to God just how good and righteous we are is a frustrating experience.

God sees us as corrupt through and through and in need of His help. God found a way to rectify our situation. It wasn't simply to overlook our problems, but rather to have His Son bear them and take upon Himself our corruption and sinfulness. God's judgment of us came upon Christ, as we see when Christ cried out on the cross, "My God, My God, why have You forsaken Me?" (Matthew 27:46). God—who has "purer eyes than to behold evil, and cannot look on wickedness" (Habakkuk 1:13)—could not look upon the sin Christ bore for us. So Christ—the perfect One standing in our place, for our wickedness—appeased God's righteous anger of our sin. When God looks on us now, He looks upon the perfect One who bore our guilt.

Some may not believe this is how it is. They imagine that sin is no big deal, and that God's love and mercy automatically overrides any hatred and judgment He has toward our sin. But think again. God isn't like us. He says, "My thoughts are not your thoughts, nor are your ways My ways" (Isaiah 55:8), and "You thought that I was altogether like you" (Psalm 50:21).

God's means for us to come to Him were visible from the beginning, as when God asked Abraham to sacrifice his son Isaac on the altar. God held back Abraham from doing this, because "God will provide for Himself the lamb" (Genesis 22:8), in place of Abraham sacrificing his son. Abraham could do nothing to seek God's favor, including sacrificing his own son; God Himself had to provide the means. Likewise, sacrificing ourselves to God will

4

not do any good; we're an imperfect sacrifice, incapable of ever meeting His demand of a perfect sacrifice for our sins.

"For in Him [Christ] dwells all the fullness of the Godhead bodily, and you are complete in Him, who is the head of all principality and power" (Colossians 2:9-10). From Old Testament times, God looked for someone among men to bring mankind back to Him, but He couldn't find that person—until He presented to us His Son. "I looked for a man among them...but I found none" (Ezekiel 22:30). We might imagine Moses as a type of that person, for he was God's choice to be the deliverer of His people from Egypt, but Moses was not that person.

On the banks of the Jordan River, after Jesus was baptized by John the Baptist, a voice came from heaven, saying, "This is My beloved Son, in whom I am well pleased" (Matthew 3:17). God presented His deliverer to redeem humanity from their despicable position. It is He alone who could cleanse us from our sin.

During the time of Moses, Israel's priests used the blood of animals to atone for the sins of the people. Only a blood sacrifice, as commanded by God, would satisfy His hatred of sin. The blood of the animals were just a symbol, a covering for them until their Savior came. When they sacrificed the blood of animals for their sins, they should have known it was an imperfect sacrifice as Paul explains in Hebrews 10:3-4: "But in those sacrifices there is a reminder of sins every year. For it is not possible that the blood of bulls and goats should take away sins." For the perfect required sacrifice for them was yet to come as Paul continues to explain in Hebrews 10:5: "Sacrifice and offering You did not desire, but a body You have prepared for Me."

Christ was what Israel had been waiting for, but a great majority of that nation did not recognize Christ as their Messiah when He came, or that He was the means by which He was going to deliver them. "He came for His own, and His own did not receive Him" (John 1:11). Not only did many of the Jews miss this, but many Gentiles did as well, which has serious consequences.

They are without excuse, because although they knew God [an inherent quality in man that God gives to see Him], they did not glorify Him as

5

> God, nor were thankful, but became futile in their thoughts, and their foolish hearts were darkened.... Therefore God gave them up to uncleanness, in the lusts of their hearts.... For this reason God gave them up to vile passions. (Romans 1:20-26)

Those who see and yet ignore God's gift of grace are giving themselves over to their natural knowledge and wisdom to navigate through life. Although most likely they'll be physically sustained by God while on earth, they'll miss out on having the kind of spiritual relationship with Him which God has intended for mankind. God deals with this rejection in a peculiar way:

> What if God, wanting to show His wrath and to make His power known, endured with much longsuffering the vessels of wrath prepared for destruction, and that He might make known the riches of His glory on the vessels of mercy, which He had prepared beforehand for glory, even us whom He called, not of the Jews only, but also of the Gentiles? (Romans 9:22-23)

God will demonstrate His power and mercy through those who accept Him, and He shows His longsuffering toward those who do not.

The world is filled with contrasts to help us see more clearly, in the physical realm as well as the spiritual realm. There was Abel, who found favor with God, and then there was Cain his brother, who did not find favor with God because his sacrifice of the fruits of his own labor were rejected. Cain, frustrated with being rejected, then killed Abel his brother.

Another contrast is the holy and righteous God set against Satan. Satan was an anointed cherub who "became filled with violence within" (Ezekiel 28:16), and who said in his heart, "I will ascend into heaven, I will exalt my throne above the stars of God; I will also sit on the mount of the congregation" (Isaiah 14:13). Do you get the picture? There are two different realms here, with no middle ground. You're either on God's side or Satan's.

You may take offense to this, but listen to how God dealt with Pharaoh, king of Egypt. Pharaoh was told by Moses to release the Israelites from his domination, but Pharaoh refused. So God sent ten plagues upon Egypt, including the death of all the firstborn sons. After enduring God's wrath, Pharaoh finally changed his mind and allowed the Israelites to go.

How foolish to try to fight against God's plan—as we see in these words to Pharaoh from God: "Indeed for this purpose I have raised you up, that I may show My power in you, and that My name may be declared in all the earth. As yet you exalt yourself against My people in that you will not let them go" (Exodus 9:16-17). God endured Pharaoh, this vessel of wrath, to make His power known to the whole world for generations to come. The Lord says, "My thoughts are not your thoughts, nor are your ways My ways" (Isaiah 55:8). God's ways are mysterious to us, but He gives us insight into how He thinks in His Word, and we need to trust Him that His light will shine on us as we read it.

CHAPTER 2

WITNESSES OF GOD

God hasn't left us in the dark about who He is, but has revealed Himself in various ways. First, there beats within every human heart an awareness that there is a God, although in some that seems to be somewhat suppressed. As we look throughout the world, people tend to worship a god in one form or other. With some intuitiveness and God's help, we should be able to see that there aren't many gods, but only one true God, and we therefore should move toward that one God. Not until an individual comes to an understanding of who God is and has accepted what He has to offer will that person feel fulfilled, as God planned it.

To help us not to be confused about who this one God is, God defined Himself in writing. "These are written that you may believe that Jesus is the Christ, the Son of God, and believing you may have life in His name" (John 20:31). John, the writer of the Gospel of John, also tells us, "The law was given through Moses, but grace and truth came through Jesus Christ. No one has seen God at any time. The only begotten Son, who is in the bosom of the Father, He has declared Him (John 1:17-18). Then we have, "All Scripture is given by inspiration of God, and is profitable for doctrine, for reproof, for correction, for instruction in righteousness, that the man of God may be complete, thoroughly equipped for every good work" (2 Timothy 3:16). The Bible become our owners manual in our understanding of God and what He expects of us. Charles Haddon Spurgeon wrote in the late 1800s about missing the revelation God has given us in His Word.

He who does not believe that God will punish sin, will not believe that He will pardon it through the atoning blood. He who does not believe that God will cast unbelievers into hell, will not be sure that He will take believers to heaven. If we doubt God's Word about one thing, we shall have small confidence in it upon another thing. Since faith in God must treat all God's Word alike; for the faith which accepts one word of God, and rejects another, is evidently not faith in God, but faith in our own judgment, faith in our own taste. I charge you who profess to be the Lord's, not to be unbelieving with regard to the terrible threatenings of God to the ungodly. Believe the threat, even though it should chill your blood; believe, though nature shrinks from the overwhelming doom, for, if you do not believe, the act of disbelieving God about one point will drive you to disbelieve Him upon the other parts of revealed truth, and you will never come to that true, childlike faith which God will accept and honor.

When Jesus left this earth He sent another witness; the Holy Spirit to commune with our spirit. The third person of the triune God moves within us to confirm that He is the true God. The Spirit of God guides us in all truth especially when reading His Word.

When He, the Spirit of truth, has come, He will guide you into all truth.....He will glorify Me, for He will take of what is Mine and declare it to you. (John 16:13-14)

The Holy Spirit is not an influence: *He* is a person, God within us. *He* is not separate from God, but works in conjunction with God the Father and God the Son to lead us in all truth, to declare and glorify God the Father to us. God gives us wisdom and understanding through His Spirit, His Word and His Son so we can know the truth. The Old Testament believers were at a disadvantage from us because many of His truths had not yet been revealed (Hebrews 1:14).

The Bible says we were created "in His own image" (Genesis 1:27). We're made in the image of God, but we aren't originals; only Christ is the original. God has given us qualities similar to Him so we can relate to who He is and be able to commune with Him. As we journey in this world we cannot know Him just because we want to know Him but need enlightenment from on high to know Him. It needs to come by grace because our natural condition lacks such perception. There are two forces working in this world, the good or godly and the evil or satanic. If our knowledge comes from an evil or worldly source, we'll follow a deceptive path and become the most miserable creatures.

God also reveals Himself through nature. Some see the world as having evolved, while others see it as God's creation. The galaxy, the mountains, streams, plant and animal life all exhibit the creative power of God. You may miss what He reveals of Himself in the physical world but you don't want to miss the revelation of Himself in the spiritual world as well. Grace gives us light to understand the story God is trying to tell us about Himself. Without this enlightenment our thoughts will put us in a dark place as seen below.

> For since the creation of the world His invisible attributes are clearly seen, being understood by the things that are made, even His eternal power and Godhead, so they are without excuse, because although they knew God, they did not glorify Him as God, nor were thankful, but became futile in their thoughts, and their foolish hearts were darkened. Professing to be wise, they became fools (Romans 1:20-22).

Besides what we talked about above God has also given us a conscience, the standard of right and wrong written on our heart. That inner voice that tells us how far short we come to meeting His standard.

Their conscience also bearing witness, and between themselves their thoughts accusing or else excusing them in the day when God will judge the secrets of men by Jesus Christ, according to my gospel. (Romans 2:15-16).

What an interesting way for God to let man know his shortfall! We need to use this invisible accuser to not drive us away from God but bring us closer to Him. So even if our conscience accuses us of horrific sins, we can repent, for "where sin abounded, grace abounded much more" (Romans 5:20). God is able to take all the wrong we've done, forgive us because of what Christ did, and then cleanse our conscience and make us free from our accuser. The shame we've experienced loses its power at the cross. Our dignity is no longer based on how we feel or what good deeds and self-sacrifices we've made, but on what He has done for us.

How much more shall the blood of Christ, who through the eternal Spirit offered Himself without spot to God, cleanse your conscience from dead works to serve the living God? (Hebrews 9:14)

Dead works being the rituals, self-sacrifices, good deeds, etc. people use to make themselves feel somewhat better about their guilty conscience and thinking maybe somehow God will tip the scales in their favor. Dead works are powerless to cleanse and set free our conscience and provide redemption.

Then there is Satan, who wants us to believe the lie that all will be well and a loving God will not punish sin—but who, at the same time, enjoys seeing us being tormented in our guilt and sin. Satan wants us to think there's no relief to our guilt, that our situation is hopeless, and that our sin is larger than His grace. Satan's weapon against us is our accusing conscience but our weapon against him is a complete trust in what Christ did to obtain forgiveness for us, no matter how disbelieving our feelings are. Without this hope, we'll have continual guilt, hopelessness, and a feeling of worthlessness.

There's a need in each one of us to take all the shame and

guilt in our life and lay it at His feet. "If we confess our sins, He is faithful and just to forgive us our sins, and to cleanse us from all unrighteousness" (1 John 1:9). The blood of Christ cleanses us from our sin, breaks down the barrier between us and God and brings us into His presence. His grace is bigger than our sin; Satan would like us to think it's the opposite.

> Man piles a mountain of sin, but God will match it, and He raises up a loftier mountain of grace; man heaps up a still larger hill of sin, but the Lord surpasses it with ten times more grace; and so the contest continues until at last the mighty God pulls up the mountains by the roots and buries man's sin beneath them as a fly might be buried beneath an Alp. Abundant sin is no barrier to the superabundant grace of God. (Grace Abounding, C. H. Spurgeon)

Jesus says: "I am the way, the truth, and the life. No one comes to the Father except through Me" (John 14:6) and "the truth shall make you free" (John 8:32). He was either the One sent to bring you to God or a great impostor, you need to decide. You may think that after you die and meet God you can plead your case or plead ignorance but listen to what the Word of God says:

> He who believes in Him is not condemned; but he who does not believe is condemned already, because he has not believed in the name of the only begotten Son of God. And this is the condemnation, that the light has come into the world, and men loved darkness rather than light, because their deeds were evil. For everyone practicing evil hates the light and does not come to the light, lest his deeds should be exposed. But he who does the truth comes to the light, that his deeds may be clearly seen, that they have been done in God. (John 3:18-21)

From this we can see that being unbelieving or noncommittal does not give us an excuse; rather, it makes us inexcusable and condemned. A commitment must take place before you die, or else it's too late—that "every mouth may be stopped, and all the world may become guilty before God" (Romans 3:19) at the judgment seat of Christ (2 Corinthians 5:10).

These revelations God has made to man show His deep concern for us. Without God's revelation of Himself man prides himself in his own righteousness, his own ingenuity, his own discoveries.

These revelations of Himself need to be understood to perceive what He is trying to tell us. If you only think God gave us a set of rules to follow and the one that obey it the best wins the prize you have it wrong. The Israelites that God redeemed from the Egyptians displeased God before the law was given. A simple trust to follow His leading would have put them on the right path. The whole Old Testament revelation was a revealing of the coming Messiah who would bring forth "grace and truth" (John 1:17). The law was concerned with the external but Christ was concerned with the internal. Apart from Christ, a sinner is in bondage to the law, a slave to sin and a captive of Satan. "Therefore if the Son makes you free, you shall be free indeed" (John 8:36).

The atheist and agnostic, who search for wisdom and understanding by their own means may feel somewhat uncomfortable with what has been said. The atheists are those who believe there's no God. The agnostics believe it's a waste of time to try to find out who God is, and they'll spend their time on other things which they deem more important. They may be powerful in this world but probably conceited, thinking they received what they have because of their own abilities and have not considered the One who gives it. The consequences of their way of thinking can be seen in Romans: "And even as they did not like to retain God in their knowledge, God gave them over to a debase mind, to do those things which are not fitting" (Romans 1:28). A debase mind has lost its capacity to think and understand what God is trying to tell them. The atheists, the agnostics, and any who do not believe or only partially believe God's Word are following a path of darkness, as we see from His Word. They were meant to worship the true God, and otherwise they'll manufacture something else to worship, like money, sex, power, or knowledge.

But God isn't frustrated with those who don't believe. In fact, He turns it around and makes them glorify Him in their unbelief. Pharaoh, king of Egypt being a good example of this. He held back the Israelites from serving God. God's answer to Pharaoh: "But indeed for this purpose I have raised you up, that I may show My power in you, and that My name may be declared in all the earth" (Exodus 9:16). God allowed Pharoah and the Egyptian people to live in a sense of freedom upon this earth until their time was up. All lives are testimonies of either living for Him or against Him.

CHAPTER 3

THE LEGALIST

It's not the do's and don'ts that that make up Christianity, but a receiving of His life into ours. Many believe that we're now on probation, that they have to prove themselves acceptable to God by their good works. Good works have their place in Christianity, but what's of utmost importance is to see our sinful condition, to come to repentance, and then to receive forgiveness and the new life Christ has to offer.

The Pharisees—the religious leaders during Jesus's time—are a good example of misinterpreting who God is and what He expected of them. They had an outward appearance of righteousness, but Jesus told them,

> Woe to you, scribes and Pharisees, hypocrites! For you are like whitewashed tombs which indeed appear beautiful outwardly, but inside are full of dead men's bones and all uncleanness. Even so you outwardly appear righteous to men, but inside you are full of hypocrisy and lawlessness. (Matthew 23:27-28)

Although they were viewed by the people of Israel as the religious teachers and leaders of their day, Jesus called them out on their hypocrisy. The Pharisees had a false sense of security in what they believed was truth, but was not. They were deceived by their own way of thinking, and actually became enslaved to it. They had a tendency to try to please God by their own competence and power, when what they needed was to come to Him with an honest heart that sees sin as sin—a heart that's able to hear, understand, and apply the message of the cross to their lives. Therefore Jesus had to say to the Pharisees, "Serpents, brood of vipers! How can you escape the condemnation of hell?" (Matthew 23:33)

Those who believe in God as the Pharisees did are deceiving themselves, thinking that by going through the right rituals they'll be good enough to get into heaven. For the Pharisees, their legalistic approach to Judaism failed to bear good fruit, and they became proud and arrogant in what they believed rather than humble and gentle.

This type of religion or thinking exists today but in a little different form. Many today think that going through the right formalities is like receiving an insurance policy, in which you pay for the policy with such things as good deeds, keeping the sacraments, reciting the creeds, attending church, ritual prayers, Bible reading, fasting, etc. They then expect to redeem that policy after they die thinking they have an entrance into heaven.

The organized church is partly responsible for this type of thinking. It's where salvation is no longer just a personal decision between you and God but a loyalty to an institution as well. The cross gets obscured by church rituals and doctrines.

We need to come to a point in our life where we realize it isn't what we do or think that brings salvation, but that God does the work in our underserving soul. A works type of religion brings only condemnation, not rewards.

The Bible talks about the fruit you bear in your life as being from either God or yourself. Jesus said, "Every tree that does not bear good fruit is cut down and thrown in the fire. Therefore by their fruits you will know them" (Matthew 7:19-20). As true believers, we derive our spiritual life from Him to bear the good fruit.

Peter tells us to "grow in the grace and the knowledge of our Lord and Savior Jesus Christ" (2 Peter 3:18). Grace is the key—it's not a doing on our part, but receiving. We need His grace even to see ourselves as He sees us—as "dead in trespasses and sins" (Ephesians 2:1).

Reading and listening to God's Word with an open heart and mind is an excellent way for Him to fill us with the knowledge of Him. Not approaching God this way will blind us to what God has for us. "For the message of the cross is foolishness to those who are perishing, but to us who are being saved it is the power of God" (1 Corinthians 1:18).

CHAPTER 4

FROM THE WILDERNESS TO THE PROMISED LAND

Having reviewed the Pharisees' wrong and legalistic approach toward worshiping God, we'll look next at three more groups who misunderstood what God was asking of them, with serious consequences.

We'll start with the descendants of Abraham, Isaac, and Jacob who were delivered by God from slavery in Egypt, then led by Him through the Red Sea and into the wilderness. These Israelites took a long walk with God that was by no means a direct path. In many ways it was a frustrating walk for both them and God, but we can learn much from their experience. Those Israelites were under the blood of the lamb, but they couldn't follow through in what they were given in a victorious way. Their worship and approach to God was seriously lacking. They lost their trust in God, to follow through what He started. They were delivered by grace, but their follow-through with God ended in a forty-year wilderness-wandering experience.

Those Israelites who were enslaved in Egypt had the faith to apply the blood of the slain lamb on their doorposts for deliverance. God opened the Red Sea for them to escape Pharaoh and his soldiers. They were led by a pillar of cloud by day and a pillar of fire by night, were given manna to eat, and were given the oracles of God, the Ten Commandments—but they lacked the faith to move on with God into the promised land, what was normally only a twelve-day journey from the Red Sea. Due to their lack of faith, God led them on a wandering path until they died in that desolate land.

This is a great example of how God deals with people who aren't in tune with Him and His plan. The wilderness wanderers' experience should awaken us who claim to be His but who may also be on such a journey. It's like trying to move forward with your car stuck in the mud; the wheels keep spinning, but the car goes nowhere. To help us get a better understanding and not get stuck in the mud, let's examine in more detail what happened, starting in Egypt. The Lord God told Moses,

> I have surely seen the oppression of *My people* who are in Egypt, and have heard their cry because of their taskmasters, for I know their sorrows. So I have come down to deliver them out of the hand of the Egyptians, and to bring them up from the land to a good and large land, to a land flowing with milk and honey. (Exodus 3:78)

You would think that by the Lord calling them "My people," they were completely protected. But let's continue.

Shortly after being delivered from the Egyptians, these people began complaining about their situation, and it was a downward spiral for them—even to the point of having Aaron make for them a calf of gold to worship. "My people" had an almost total disconnect from their God. By having Aaron make them a golden calf, they distorted and corrupted the character of God into something with no deliverable qualities. The idea of worshiping a golden calf may have come from their remembering the pagan worship of the bull god Apis back in Egypt. The wilderness wanderers ended up worshiping the god of this world rather than putting their trust in the hands of the true God.

We then see God's reaction to the Israelites, while Moses was on Mount Sinai receiving the Ten Commandments:

> The Lord said to Moses, "Go, get down! For *your people* whom you brought out of the land of Egypt

have corrupted themselves. They have turned aside quickly out of the way which I commanded them. They have made themselves a molded calf, and worshiped it and sacrificed to it, and said, 'This is your god, O Israel, that brought you out of the land of Egypt!'" And the Lord said to Moses, "I have seen this people, and indeed it is a stiff-necked people! Now therefore, let Me alone, that My wrath may burn hot against them and I may consume them. And I will make of you a great nation." (Exodus 32:7-10)

God's anger against the Israelites may seem extreme, even to the point of wanting to annihilate them from the face of the earth and start over again with descendants of Moses. In speaking earlier to Moses, God had referred to these Israelites as "My people"; but now, speaking again to Moses, in His anger He calls them "your people."

Only Moses at this point in history was able to turn away God's wrath and mediate between God and the Israelites. Do you think any of those Israelites who worshiped the golden calf would have that kind of persuasive power with God?

God deals with people differently today than He did in Old Testament times, but His feelings toward His people when they do wrong has not changed. Fortunately, we have Christ as our Mediator to go to for forgiveness and reconciliation, and our conscience and the Holy Spirit convict us of wrong to bring us to repentance. This Old Testament account gives us a picture of how God feels about us when we sin, and also how someone can stand in the gap and reconcile us back to Him.

Because of their unfaithfulness, those Israelites did not have the wherewithal to move on with God into the promised land. They had the initial blessing of God, but they couldn't take the next step. Not taking that next step with God meant just going through the ritualistic motions of being an Israelite and wandering in the wilderness until you die. It wasn't that God couldn't bring them into the promised land, but that He wouldn't reward their unbelief.

This brings a warning for us: "Therefore, since a promise remains of entering His rest [promised-land rest for the Israelites, and a spiritual rest for us], let us fear lest any of *you* seem to come short of it" (Hebrews 4:1). What held back the Israelites from taking that next step may also be inherent in us. To move into His rest, we need a total commitment of our life to Him, something the Israelites did not have.

The next generation of Israelites did go into the promised land. The challenge for that generation was that God gave them the land, but before they received it they were required to drive out the inhabitants who were already there. Basically this was the same challenge given to their forefathers. They had to decide—with their mind and will—to move forward with God. They needed to see what their forefathers failed to see, and have the fortitude to carry out that vision.

For us to move on with God, we need to see what we have in Christ that overcomes sin and drives the enemy out of our life.

That next generation that crossed the Jordan and entered the promised land had the confidence, courage, and determination to conquer Jericho. They marched around the walls of Jericho seven days. And then, when the command was given, they blew their horns and shouted. The result was that the walls of Jericho came tumbling down, and Israel conquered Jericho. They fought the battle God's way and were successful.

Sometimes we have a problem bringing down the walls in our life that inhibit our relationship with God, but maybe it's because we're relying on our own way of doing things rather than His.

With their next challenge, at the city of Ai, the people of Israel were quickly met with defeat. God explained to them the reason:

> Israel has sinned, and they have also transgressed My covenant which I have commanded them. For they have even taken some of the accursed things [earlier, from Jericho], and have both stolen and deceived; and they have also put it among their own stuff. Therefore the children of Israel could not stand before their enemies, but turned their backs before their enemies, because they have become

doomed to destruction. Neither will I be with you
anymore, unless you destroy the accursed from
among you. (Joshua 7:11-12)

Having unconfessed sin before God is a serious problem.
Understanding Israel's situation here can help us avoid defeat in
our life.

Sin was at the forefront of Israel's problem, and God cannot
overlook sin. He had previously stated, "And you, by all means
abstain from the accursed things, lest you become accursed when
you take of the accursed things, and make the camp of Israel a
curse, and trouble it" (Joshua 6:18). At Jericho, God required all
the spoils of war to be His, but one man selfishly kept something
for himself. This act of disobedience not only brought judgment
upon himself and his family, but also jeopardized the whole nation
of Israel.

The Lord's reaction seems extreme, but it stems from His
hatred of sin as seen in Deuteronomy 6:15— "The Lord your God
is a jealous God among you, lest the anger of the Lord your God
be aroused against you and destroy you from the face of the
earth." The application for us today is this: If we have unconfessed
sin, the Lord's anger is aroused against us. The Lord's nature
hasn't changed since Old Testament times. He's still a jealous God
and may withhold from us spiritual rest if there's some sin or
disobedience in our life. God may not destroy us off the face of
the earth as He almost did with the Israelites, but the consequence
of losing some fellowship and peace with Him is grievous.

The Israelite warriors feared by the nations of Canaan now
lost their courage and "fled before the men at Ai" (Joshua 7:4).
We, too, may lose courage and confidence because we aren't right
with God, and it just might be because of unconfessed or hidden
sins in our life.

God would no longer be with Israel until they dealt with
the problem. Could we, too, lose our fellowship and peace with
God because some "accursed thing" has not been put away? God
desires that nothing come between us. This applies not only to
individuals but to the body of believers as well.

> Now all these things happened to them as examples,
> and they were written for our admonition, upon
> whom the ends of the ages have come. Therefore
> let him who thinks he stands take heed lest he fall.
> (1 Corinthians 10:11-12)

As we examine ourselves, we cannot overlook the end of this verse: "Let him who thinks he stands take heed less he fall." The Israelites may have been somewhat self-confident, like the Pharisees in their belief, but blind to what God actually required of them. We as Christians are under the blood of the Lamb as the Israelites were: "For indeed Christ, our Passover, was sacrificed for us" (1 Corinthians 5:7). We may say we're standing on what we have in Christ, yet not be aware of how in some way may be displeasing God. The Israelites at Ai went forward into battle without realizing there was hidden sin in the camp and they were sorely defeated. There was victory at Jericho, but they were beaten at Ai because of hidden sin. After the sin was confessed and dealt with, Israel moved forward with God, conquering most of the land God had for them.

Of those Israelites in the wilderness, we read, "Again and again they tempted God, and limited the Holy One of Israel" (Psalm 78:41). The land flowing with milk and honey could have been quickly possessed, but the people couldn't claim their blessing or put their lives into God's hands.

We need to see the promise God has for us and claim our blessing. The "love, joy, peace, longsuffering, gentleness, goodness, faith, meekness, temperance" (Galatians 5:22-23 kjv)—all this is ours, all of it given at salvation and waiting to be claimed. We cannot afford to allow worldly activities to blind us of the opportunities God has for us. "Where there is no vision, the people perish" (Proverbs 29:18 kjv)—a perishing like that of those in the wilderness, who had no vision of God's expectation of them.

CHAPTER 5

PROFESSED CHRISTIAN SLAVEHOLDERS

We'll look next at another group who failed God—the Christian slaveholders of the American South during the 1700s and 1800s. This involved a bit of a different situation from the Israelites in Egypt, who were slaves and set free from pagan masters. But in the South, these were supposedly Christian people who held slaves, and in countless cases abused them. All these groups we're discussing appear to have godly fears and good intentions, but they miss what God has for them. The consequences of one's actions are clearly seen in history. The wilderness wanderers did not follow through with God to go into the promised land, and we'll see in this chapter how these Christians of the American South will go to war in order to keep their practice of slavery.

Slavery was an entrenched part of the culture in the South at this time, and the question arises: How did God look upon these apparent Christian slaveholders? Although many claimed to live by the golden rule— "Whatever you want men to do to you, do also to them" (Matthew 7:12)—their actions didn't show that. Were these people God's people or not? That's a tough question that only God can answer, but there's a warning here for us to not fall into their way of thinking.

They were an embarrassment to Christianity, to say the least. God gave them a conscience to make them aware of what they were doing, and they'll have to answer for their behavior. When we're in a state of denial, it's easy to rely on our own thoughts and prejudices to excuse our behavior. These slaveholders may even have relied on Scripture to justify their actions. They probably reasoned, "If slavery existed during Jesus's time, we also have this God-given right." They must have missed what Scripture says in Malachi 2:10 about treating our fellow human beings:

> Have we not all one Father? Has not one God created us? Why do we deal treacherously with one another by profaning the covenant of the fathers?

To understand this situation better, let's look first at what some in the South were saying at this time.

> [Slavery] was established by decree of Almighty God...it is sanctioned in the Bible, in both Testaments, from Genesis to Revelation...it has existed in all ages, has been found among the people of the highest civilization, and in nations of the highest proficiency in the arts. (Jefferson Davis, president of the Confederate States of America)

> The right of holding slaves is clearly established in the Holy Scriptures, both by precept and example. (Richard Furman, president of the South Carolina Baptist Convention)

In the 1840s to 1860s, the major Christian denominations in the United States split over the issue of slavery, dividing them into northern and southern entities. The Methodist Episcopal Church split in 1844; in 1845 the Baptists officially separated; then in 1861, the Presbyterian Church divided. A quotation from a Presbyterian meeting in Georgia shows slavery to be the main issue.

> It is not to be disguised that the North exercises a deep and settled antipathy [a deep-seated feeling of dislike] to slavery itself, while the South is equally zealous in its defense. Recent events can have no other effect than to confirm the antipathy on the one hand and strengthen the attachment on the

other. (from the Minutes of the General Assembly of the Presbyterian Church in the Confederate States of America, Augusta, Georgia, 1861)

Let's face it. The main driving force for church slaveholders was to make money, to increase their land holdings, to make their own life easier, and to gain some prominence in their community. All these motives were for self-interest, no matter how much they used the Bible to justify their action. Without the truth you open yourself up to deception, and the Adversary can fill you with many different ideas and prejudices, such as thinking something is the truth when in fact it opposes God. Had these slaveholders not thought of the destruction they caused to the slave families, from the time they were captured and then through the highly dangerous voyages bringing them to North America? The slave trade existed because there was a demand for cheap labor to work in the fields. For these churchgoers to biblically justify their actions was absurd.

Before the Civil War began, Harriet Beecher Stowe wrote her novel *Uncle Tom's Cabin*. When Abraham Lincoln met her, he reportedly said, "So you're the little woman who wrote the book that made this great war!" The main point of her novel was centered around these words: "Ye are come to Mount Zion, and unto the city of the living God" (Hebrews 12:22 kjv), referring to all Christians, which included black Christians as well. The author inferred that if a slave can come to Mount Zion and to Jesus and to a company of saints in the New Jerusalem, how can you set him up on an auction block and trade him from one white man to another? This woman questioned the status quo at the time, and she heightened people's awareness of what was going on in the South. Although her warnings were generally ignored in the South itself, it should have been their wakeup call.

Let us now look at the so-called Christian slaveholder from a slave's point of view. Frederick Douglass was born a slave in 1818 in the South, escaped from slavery in 1838, and later became an internationally renowned abolitionist and orator. He also had a long association with the women's rights movement. During the Civil War, President Lincoln called upon him for advice on emancipation issues.

Douglass writes the following:

> I assert most unhesitatingly, that the religion of the South is a mere covering for the most horrid crimes—a justifier of the most appalling barbarity—a sanctifier of the most hateful frauds—and a dark shelter under which the darkest, foulest, grossest, and most infernal deeds of slaveholders find the strongest protection. Were I to be again reduced to the chains of slavery, next to that enslavement, I should regard being the slave of a religious master the greatest calamity that could befall me. For of all slaveholders with whom I have ever met, religious slaveholders are the worst. (from *Narrative of the Life of Frederick Douglass, an American Slave, Written by Himself*)

In the same book, Douglas goes in more detail about his experiences:

> In August, 1832, my master (Captain Auld) attended a Methodist camp-meeting held in the Bay-side, Talbot county, and there experienced religion. I indulged a faint hope that his conversion would lead him to emancipate his slaves, and that, if he did not do this, it would, at any rate, make him more kind and humane. I was disappointed in both these respects. It neither made him to be humane to his slaves, nor to emancipate them. If it had any effect on his character, it made him more cruel and hateful in all his ways; for I believe him to have been a much worse man after his conversion than before. Prior to his conversion, he relied upon his own depravity to shield and sustain him in his savage barbarity; but after his conversion, he found religious sanction and support for his slaveholding cruelty. He made

the greatest pretensions to piety. His house was the house of prayer. He prayed morning, noon, and night. He very soon distinguished himself among his brethren, and was soon made a class-leader and exhorter. His activity in revivals was great, and he proved himself an instrument in the hands of the church in converting many souls. His house was the preachers' home. They used to take great pleasure in coming there to put up; for while he starved us, he stuffed them. We have had three or four preachers there at a time.

The question we should ask at this point is: How does one who is forgiven by God for his sins, and supposedly has been given a new nature, inflict such pain on fellow human beings?

Occurrences like these were happening all over the South, and to some degree in the North as well, under the eye of the Christian church, with hardly any protest in the South. Why such blindness and inaction? Apparently the church leaders and the politicians supported slavery, and the people followed.

Some people believe truth is whatever has been made clear to them in their own mind, but we can be easily deceived, because our natural, prideful mind and heart will allow that deception. Scripture says, "The carnal [fleshly or natural] mind is enmity against God" (Romans 8:7), so we cannot always trust what our mind has concluded. To accentuate the problem, our natural perspective or opinion often gets outside information to support what we already think. We pick and choose information to support what we want our conclusion to be. The Bible can be used to support our conclusions; if the words agree with our point of view we accept it and use it for more confirmation on what we believe; if the Bible disagrees, we reject its testimony.

The so-called Christian slaveholder's wrongful behavior may seem radical—but doesn't this same nature lie dormant in all of us, waiting for the opportunity to rear its ugly head in different ways?

The works of the flesh are evident, which are: adultery, fornication, uncleanness, lewdness, idolatry, hatred, contentions, jealousies, outbursts of wrath, selfish ambitions, dissensions, heresies, envy, murders, drunkenness, revelries, and the like; of which I tell you beforehand, just as I also told you in time past, that those who practice such things will not inherit the kingdom of God. (Galatians 5:19-21)

Strong and fearful words: "Those who practice such things will not inherit the kingdom of God." Those so-called Christian slaveholders may have had strong convictions about their salvation, and they have thought they were right and even righteous, but we wouldn't want to be in their shoes on the day of judgment.

The Son of Man will send out His angels, and they will gather out of His kingdom all things that offend, and those who practice lawlessness, and will cast them into the furnace of fire. There will be wailing and gnashing of teeth. (Matthew 13:41-42)

Slavery is offensive, and the evidence seems to be stacked against slaveholders. But who knows? Only God can judge and know what is in a man's heart. If the South repented earlier of this practice, they might have avoided the Civil War, which took the lives of 620,000 soldiers, plus many civilian casualties. England was able to abolish slavery by peaceful means in 1833, but the United States was judged harshly for their lack of repentance. Even after the war, prejudice against the blacks continued. Apparently many never owed up to their sin, which says much about their Christianity, if they really were Christians at all.

If we truly receive God's life by the blood sacrifice of Christ, that sin nature we inherited from Adam and Eve can be held in check, but never gotten rid of. Without the overriding power of the Holy Spirit, we won't see clearly or deal properly with our natural life. You may put on a show of being a true Christian, like those so-called Christian slaveholders, but "do not be deceived, God is not mocked; for whatever a man sows, that he will also reap"

(Galatians 6:7). Many of those so-called Christian slaveholders may have claimed to have the same mind in them that was in Christ Jesus, as stated in 1 Corinthians 2:16: "We have the mind of Christ"—which is unimaginable in their case, but they seem not to have realized this. And what could those slaves have thought about Christianity when they went through such ordeals and sufferings from their masters?

The grace that had been given to those so-called Christian slaveholders and supporters of slavery was something they failed to apply to their fellow man. They became slaves to their own way of thinking, and "walked according to the course of this world" (Ephesians 2:2).

We could all use some self-introspection regarding what we think is right, so we don't fall under false pretenses, thinking everything's all right when it isn't. We need to be cautious in the way we think, because we were all born with a natural mind and heart that is selfish and tends to conflict with God's ways.

CHAPTER 6

GERMAN CHRISTIANS DURING HITLER'S REIGN

This last group we'll look at as having questionable Christian genuineness are those professed Christians who helped Hitler come to power. After coming to power, Hitler not only started a world war but tried to wipe out all Jews from the face of the earth.

The point in bringing up these religious groups—the Pharisees, the Israelites in the wilderness, the so-called Christian slaveholders in the American South, and now these professing Christians who supported Hitler—is for us to be careful to avoid the traps Satan sets for us in our generation. To avoid whatever diversion Satan and the world has to offer, we need to stay focused on the things that are of upmost importance to God.

Have you ever played a sport using a bat, racket, or paddle to hit a small ball? You come to realize that keeping your eye on that ball before you hit it is of upmost importance. It's the same with Christianity. What is of most importance to God?

With that in mind, let's look at the Christian church in Germany during the 1930s, as it fell into a wrong way of thinking. While Hitler was rising to power, Germany's Christian church was basically Lutheran. Adolf Hitler started by influencing German politics, and the German people were generally pleased with what he was doing. The country was ripe for a person like Hitler. They'd been humiliated after their defeat in World War 1, there were many financial burdens put on them to repay other countries for the damage caused in World War 1, their currency collapsed, they were emotionally downtrodden, and the world was going through a depression, with people starving. Hitler seemed to be someone who could get the country going again, and in the process give the German people back their pride and dignity. The German people were caught up in supporting something that appeared good for the nation and the church, but in the end they compromised their Christian principles.

Not having good spiritual insight can easily give way to wrong thinking.

Hitler addressed the Christian community by telling them he would respect their rights and would make "a peaceful accord between church and state" (as William L. Shirer writes in *The Rise and Fall of the Third Reich*). With this assurance, the masses felt comfortable, because Hitler stressed "freedom" and "peace" for the German people as well as for the churches—just what they wanted to hear. The German Protestant church, basically Lutheran during this time, was asked by Hitler to join him in a quest to unify Germany into a strong and prominent nation once again.

While gaining the people's trust, Hitler was able to gain more power by becoming chancellor of a coalition government in January of 1933. In February of that year, the building that housed the German Reichstag (legislature) was suspiciously destroyed by fire. In March, the so-called Enabling Act was passed making Hitler a virtual dictator. Hitler called for martial law for the protection of the people and the state, thus dissolving the existing democratic system. He then abolished freedom of speech and freedom of the press. While two-thirds of the Protestant church supported Hitler, the other third did not, but they suffered grave consequences. As time went on, much of the so-called Christian church continued to stand behind Hitler even when he began persecuting the Jews. Hitler stressed that the Jews were getting what they deserved for crucifying the Savior of the world, Jesus Christ.

Here is a letter from a Christian pastor complementing Hitler on his stand:

> We stand enthusiastically behind your struggle against the Jewish death watch beetles which are

undermining our German nations…. So too against those friends of Jewry which are found even in the ranks of the Protestant pastorate. We will fight alongside you and will not give up until the struggle against all Jewry and against the murderers of Our Savior has been brought to a victorious end, in the Spirit of Christ and of Martin Luther.

In true fellowship, I greet you with Heil Hitler.
Pastor Riechelmann

How do you explain such a letter from a pastor of a Christian church?

Dietrich Bonhoeffer was a pastor who opposed Hitler and warned the Christian community by saying, "We Lutherans have gathered like eagles around the carcass of cheap grace, and there we have drunk the poison which has killed the life of following Christ." He continues:

Cheap grace is the deadly enemy of our Church. We are fighting today for costly grace…. In such a church, the world finds a cheap covering for its sins; no contrition is required, still less any real desire to be delivered from sin…. Cheap grace means the justification of the sinner…. It is grace without discipleship, grace without the cross, grace without Jesus Christ, living and incarnate. (from *The Cost of Discipleship*)

Dietrich Bonhoeffer was executed by the German authorities in a concentration camp two weeks before the camp was liberated by Allied forces.

Did many of those professed Christians in Germany who supported Hitler really know Christ and the grace that should have been given them? Apparently they didn't see the hypocrisy in their lives, and they'll be judged on what they believed.

We need the wisdom of the Holy Spirit so that we don't fall into similar errors.

> Examine yourselves as to whether you are in the faith. Test yourselves. Do you not know yourselves, that Jesus Christ is in you?—unless you are indeed disqualified. But I trust that you will know that we are not disqualified. (2 Corinthians 13:56)

When Christ is not the center of our life, or not the center of the church, many horrible problems can arise. Even when our lives are based on seemingly good sacramental, political, or philosophical agendas, without Christ being at the forefront of everything, we're unstable.

Those groups we've mentioned so far were like carts that ran with wheels off center, "tossed to and fro and carried about with every wind of doctrine, by the trickery of men, in the cunning craftiness of deceitful plotting" (Ephesians 4:14). A mindset is needed that doesn't compromise our biblical principles—no matter the situation, no matter the consequences. A critical assessment of ourselves regarding whether we have the Christian graces He has provided will help us understand where we are.

CHAPTER 7

WHEAT AND TARES

In the parable given by Jesus in Matthew 13:24-30, we see that there are wheat and tares in the church—the wheat being the true Christians, the tares being those merely professing to be Christians. When the servants of the owner of the field were aware that the enemy had sown tares among the wheat, they asked the landowner if they could gather up the tares. The owner said, "No, lest while you gather up the tares you also uproot the wheat with them. Let both grow together until the harvest" (Matthew 13:29-30).

One message from this is that the difference between the two is so slight, it's almost impossible to distinguish between them. If these servants pulled up the tares, they might mistakenly pull up some wheat as well. When Jesus interprets this parable, He says this:

> The enemy who sowed them is the devil, the harvest is the end of the age, and the reapers are the angels. Therefore as the tares are gathered and burned in the fire, so it will be at the end of the age. The Son of Man will send out His angels, and they will gather out of His kingdom all things that offend, and those who practice lawlessness, and will cast them into the furnace of fire. There will be wailing and gnashing of teeth. (Matthew 13:39-42)

The tares' identity is at first indistinguishable from that of the wheat, but will be disclosed at the end of the age and dealt with.

Satan wants to destroy the witness of the wheat, so he scatters the tares among them. The "wheat" doesn't not know who the "tares" are, but Satan also keep the tares ignorant of their own condition, to a certain extent. This explains why some in the past who claimed to be believers acted as they did. For "the god of this age"—Satan—has blinded the minds of those who don't believe, as Paul explains in 2 Corinthians 4:4. Not only are the tares blinded about what they believe is truth, but "the whole world lies under the sway of the wicked one" (1 John 5:19).

Satan's goal is to keep all his own in their ignorant state. Paul tells true believers to "no longer walk as the rest of the Gentiles walk, in the futility of their mind, having their understanding darkened, being alienated from the life of God, because of the ignorance that is in them, because of the blindness of their heart" (Ephesians 4:18).

Some of those people we've been discussing had false interpretations of the Bible, prejudices, and a wrong thinking about God. They were being held in darkness, incapable of seeing the true light. Even true believers can be deceived, and they need to pay close attention as they read the Word to gain "an understanding, that we may know Him that is true," on this basis: "We are in Him who is true, in His Son Jesus Christ" (1 John 5:20). The truth given by the Spirit of God can defeat the works of the evil one and lift the veil of darkness over our hearts.

Satan is happy for the tares to please themselves and fulfill their earthly desires, as long as they don't realize the source of their deception. Those five virgins were shocked when the door was closed for them. And what about those who thought they did well only to hear the words from Jesus: "I never knew you"? They were shocked because their self-perception was so different from how God perceived them.

Many tares don't realize that their natural corrupt human nature is deceiving them, blinding them of the truth, and even making them think everything's all right when it isn't. Satan wants us in that position, for he "has blinded their eyes and hardened their hearts, lest they should see with their eyes, lest they should understand with their hearts and turn, so that I (God) should heal them" (John 12:40). The tares may appear to others to be upright people, but they're lacking His life and the full assurance that God gives to His true children.

CHAPTER 8

WISDOM AND UNDERSTANDING

We now proceed to see where we should be in order to not be merely professing Christians, but Christians who demonstrate the Christian attributes of love, joy, peace, longsuffering, and more.

To begin, let's look at something written by Solomon, David's son: "Happy is the man who finds wisdom, and the man who gains understanding…. She [wisdom] is a tree of life to those who take hold of her, and happy are all who retain her" (Proverbs 3:13-18). Wisdom and understanding are "a tree of life," but not *the* Tree of Life. Christ Himself is the true Tree of Life, as represented in the tree that was guarded by the cherubim in the garden of Eden, after Adam and Eve ate of the "tree of knowledge of good and evil" (Genesis 3:6; 3:24).

We have inherited from Adam the fruits of the tree of knowledge of good and evil, and we need to override that with fruit from the tree of life. The fruit from the tree of life gives us wisdom and understanding and access to God. We have an old nature in us that's corrupt, so we need the "tree of life" not only for salvation, but for wisdom and understanding as well. Many have a partial understanding of God and lack much because they haven't fed on the wisdom and understanding from the tree of life.

> If you seek her [wisdom] as silver,
> and search for her as hidden treasure;
> then you will understand the fear of the Lord,
> and find the knowledge of God. (Proverbs 2:45)

Forgiveness and deliverance from sin is the basis for us to have an authentic walk with God, but we need to ask how we can we *walk* with someone so unlike ourselves. In the Old Testament, it's said of Enoch and Noah that they "walked with God" (Genesis 5:24, 6:9). The Old Testament prophet Amos said, "Can two walk together, except they are agreed?" (Amos 3:3). Those Old Testament saints were in agreement with God and walked with Him.

Another example of one who had a walk with God was Moses. He was an Israelite whom God molded into the person He wanted him to be. The result of God's undertaking is seen in these words: "So the Lord spoke to Moses face to face, as a man speaks to his friend" (Exodus 33:11). The Lord spoke and guided Moses to lead the children of Israel in the wilderness for forty years. Christ in us enables us to walk with Him just as Enoch, Noah, Moses, and Amos did, but we must also go through trials and tribulations.

When we were born anew by God, we obtained full salvation, but we lacked the full knowledge of what took place. As we "grow in the grace and knowledge of our Lord and Savior Jesus Christ" (2 Peter 3:18), we become more aware of what God has given us. We need to make ourselves available and to heed these words: "Be diligent to present yourself to God, a worker who does not need to be ashamed, rightly dividing the word of truth" (2 Timothy 2:15).

The Old Testament prophet Hosea conveyed these words from God to Israel: "My people are destroyed for lack of knowledge. Because you have rejected knowledge, I also will reject you" (Hosea 4:6). God is making the point that the people of Israel are destroyed spiritually because they lacked true knowledge. The Jewish leaders and priests and the people of Hosea's time not only lacked knowledge, but actively rejected it.

Without true knowledge, our situation is dire, resulting in a quenched relationship with God instead of a close walk with Him.

In the book of Revelation, Jesus gave this message to the church at Ephesus: "To him who overcomes I will give to eat from the tree of life, which is in the midst of the Paradise of God" (Revelation 2:7). We become overcomers by allowing the Spirit of grace to work in our lives. These are the ones whose affections and obedience toward God come first in their lives. No human wisdom, no philosophy, and no reasoning will demonstrate the

Christian virtues in our life without the power of the Spirit of God working in us. "That which is born of the flesh is flesh, and that which is born of the Spirit is spirit" (John 3:6). The Lord says:

> Let not the wise man glory in his wisdom, nor let the mighty man glory in his might, nor let the rich man glory in his riches; but let him who glories glory in this, that he understands and knows Me. (Jeremiah 9:23-24)

God's intention is that we know and understand Him, and we therefore need wisdom and knowledge from the "tree of life" to do it.

When we don't possess the truth, this gives our enemy fertile ground to debilitate us. "Be sober, be vigilant; because your adversary the devil walks about like a roaring lion, seeking whom he may devour" (1 Peter 5:8). When the predator Satan looks for prey, he usually will look for the weakest to attack. A twisted and perverted approach to religion provides footing for evil spirits to work, further removing them from God's truth.

When Christ came to the Jews, there were many upstanding Jews who worshiped in the temple, and studied the Scriptures, and sought to keep the law; but they were blinded to who Christ was. They lacked true knowledge and were prideful about what they believed to be right.

The Pharisees attempted to live in a constant state of purity while lacking true knowledge. They had a false sense of assurance with self-righteousness disguised in humility, as seen in the parable of the Pharisee and the tax collector, something Jesus spoke "to some who trusted in themselves that they were righteous, and despised others"—

> Two men went up to the temple to pray, one a Pharisee and the other a tax collector. The Pharisee stood and prayed thus with himself, "God, I thank You that I am not like other men—extortioners, unjust, adulterers,

or even as this tax collector. I fast twice a week; I give tithes of all I possess." (Luke 18:10-12).

Here the word "I" is used five times in just two sentences—showing how they trusted in their own righteousness without realizing their depravity. The Pharisees didn't understand that they were as sinful as others. When following the law, they were deceived into thinking they were righteous in themselves and deserved an entrance into heaven, while in reality they were following their father the devil (John 8:44). They merely "trusted in themselves that they were righteous" (Luke 18:9).

Meanwhile the tax collector prayed in a different manner: "God, be merciful to me a sinner!" (Luke 18:13) The tax collector had a humble position before God, not an exalted position like that of the Pharisee. He realized that "all have sinned and fall short of the glory of God" (Romans 3:23).

Many Jews were full of admiration and praise when Jesus entered Jerusalem riding on a donkey. The multitude cried out, "Hosanna to the Son of David! Blessed is He who comes in the name of the Lord!" (Matthew 21:9). They seemed to be true followers of Christ. But only days later, were they essentially the same crowd as the "multitudes" influenced by Christ's enemies? "The chief priests and elders persuaded the multitudes that they should ask for Barabbas and destroy Jesus" (Matthew 27:20). That emotional crowd lacked true knowledge, and they compelled the governor by shouting, "Let Him be crucified" (Matthew 27:22).

Emotions often come from our flesh, and they can express worship and love for Christ at one moment while sparking ungodly actions the next. Emotions can be genuine, but without much knowledge and depth, they're meaningless.

Paul the apostle, a Pharisee himself, expressed how many of the Jews were emotionally attached to God: "They have a zeal for God, but not according to knowledge" (Romans 10:2).

"Religious" minded people are easily susceptible to wrong thinking. Many of these people we've discussed so far thought they were right, but they became slaves to their own way of thinking and "walked according to the course of this world" (Ephesians 2:2) without even realizing it.

And remember this: In their worship of God, the Pharisees, the so-called Christian slaveholders, and those who supported Hitler may have studied more of Scripture than many professing Christians today—this should bring great trepidation.

CHAPTER 9

THE ADVERSARY

So who or what prevents us from obtaining true wisdom and understanding for a closer walk with Him?

We can blame it on the world's temptations, or on our natural desires going against godly principles, or on Satan's influential power over us. But in the end, the blame is put personally on us. All those distractions must be dealt with. In this chapter we'll discuss how the great deceiver of our souls can turn us away from God. For God desires His people to be "conformed to the image of His Son" (Romans 8:29), and we must realize we are weak in ourselves and need Him to accomplish this.

Satan who is very tenacious wants us conformed to his image and will go to great lengths to accomplish this. Since we never get rid of our sin nature he tries to make our natural desires a playground for him to work with. But God has provided the means to overcome the Adversary.

In our unregenerate state we had a heart for the world—Satan's world—and godly things seemed foolish to us.

> And you He made alive, who were dead in trespasses and sins, in which you once walked according to the course of this world, according to the prince of the air [Satan], the spirit who now works in the sons of disobedience, among whom also we *all* once conducted ourselves in the lust of the flesh, fulfilling the desires of the flesh and of

the mind, and were by nature children of wrath,
just as the others. (Ephesians 2:12)

Regeneration doesn't totally protect us against Satan's influence, especially since we retain our old nature. We now have the ability to deal with Satan, but God allows Satan to test us, just as he allowed Satan to test Jesus. If God permitted, Satan could sift us as wheat, as seen in the words about that spoken by Jesus to Peter in Luke 22:31. God's pleasure for us as believers is not for us to fail under Satan's temptations, but to be strengthened in Him by the trial.

One of our natural inclinations is to fear when trials and tests come. This fear can easily overtake us if we allow it. Resting in Christ is our only true weapon in our resistance against Satan and our natural desires. Many of those persons we previously looked at appeared to rest in their own strength, and they failed the trials and tests set before them. God uses trials to help us (and others) to see the condition of our heart, and to show us how dependent we are on Him to get through this life. These trials can either bring us closer to God or separate us from Him.

Job's severe example in this regard is instructive.

There was a man in the land of Uz, whose name was Job; and that man was blameless and upright, and one who feared God and shunned evil…. Then the Lord said to Satan, "Have you considered My servant Job, that there is none like him on the earth, a blameless and upright man, one who fears God and shuns evil?" …And the Lord said to Satan, "Behold, he is in your hand, but spare his life." (Job 1:1, 8; 2:6)

God loved Job, but Satan was permitted to try him. This trial of suffering in the end produced a more Christlike character which was pleasing to God. If God allowed His testing to afflict Job, "a blameless and upright man," then how will we escape such trials? We need to be fully dependent on Him and have His life, His knowledge, and His power in our life to deal with the tests and trials He sets before us. Without Him, we deal with Satan in our own strength and set ourselves up for failure.

The apostle Paul went through many trials, and he speaks of the strength he received from God:

> And my speech and my preaching were not with persuasive words of human wisdom, but in demonstration of the Spirit and of power, that your faith should not be in the wisdom of men but in the power of God. (1 Corinthians 2:4-5)

Paul goes on:

> Even so no one knows the things of God except the Spirit of God. Now we have received, not the spirit of the world, but the Spirit who is from God, that we might know the things freely given to us by God. These things we also speak, not in words which man's wisdom teaches but which the Holy Spirit teaches, comparing spiritual things with spiritual. But the natural man does not receive the things of the Spirit of God, for they are foolishness to him; nor can he know them, because they are spiritually discerned. (1 Corinthians 2:11-14)

The enemy, Satan, knows our situation and seeks to draw us away from God. Satan can cause much confusion in our minds about salvation and the new life God has given us. Some of Satan's schemes are obvious, but there are many things he does under the cover of darkness.

We expect the unregenerate to be deceived, but we whose sins have been forgiven may think we're protected from such deception, and that Satan can penetrate us only so far, if that. Before Paul's conversion he lived under the influence of Satan (Ephesians 2:13) although he thought otherwise. He described himself as "a Hebrew of the Hebrews...concerning the righteousness which is in the law, blameless" (Philippians 3:56). Even Peter, who was converted, fell into deception and had to be reprimanded by Christ and then later by Paul. Peter and Paul were both apostles, yet Paul "withstood him [Peter] to his face, because he was to be blamed" (Galatians 2:11). So we, too, need to be cautious and alert not to fall into deception, even at times when we feel the most confident.

"Now the Spirit expressly says that in latter times some will depart from the faith, giving heed to deceiving spirits and doctrines of demons" (1 Timothy 4:1). Many think we're now living in those "latter times," and as we get closer to the end Satan will be busier than ever, knowing his time is short. Eve, who had no sin nature, fell into the trap of Satan, who told her this lie: "You will not surely die. For God knows that in the day you eat of it your eyes will be opened, and you will be like God, knowing good and evil" (Genesis 3:45). His deceptive ways are very appealing to our emotions, as they were to Eve. Satan comes to us not as a despicable character, but "transforms into an angel of light" (1 Corinthians 11:14).

Let's take the concept of hell. When was the last time you heard a sermon on that subject? It's an important part of the message God is trying to get across, but it isn't mentioned much because apparently it might put God in a bad light—having people suffer for eternity. If Satan gets that left out of the message, he'll try to remove other things also, or twist the Bible message to give it a different meaning. He'll also isolate portions of Scripture to change the true meaning in the context.

The supposedly Christian slaveholders used Scripture to justify their cruel practice of slavery, as did many others to justify their cruel treatment of individuals. The great deceiver through the ages has had many years of experience substituting falsehoods for the truth.

Let's admit it: We, too, fall into deception like Eve, because we rely on our own wisdom and reasoning. We may even think our conclusions are coming from the Holy Spirit when they may not be. We're told to test the spirits, to discern between "the spirit of truth and the spirit of error" (1 John 4:6). The Pharisees claimed to have God as their Father, but Jesus called them "fools and blind" (Matthew 23:17), and "full of hypocrisy and lawlessness" (Matthew 23:28). Satan's goal for unbelievers is much the same for believers—to keep them stuck "in the futility of their mind, having their understanding darkened, being alienated from the life of God, because of the ignorance that is in them" (Galatians 4:17-18).

Another important point to bring out is that the Holy Spirit gives wisdom to those who desire to part with their sins. Apparently some of those we've discussed were not willing to do that, and they were led deeper along their destructive path.

After Jesus fasted for forty days, Satan's objective for Him was to make Him sin. Isn't his objective the same for us? Even after we're saved and forgiven of our sins, Satan's objective for us is to keep us sinning. If we fall into sin after being regenerated, we have an even more uncomfortable feeling, because we have a heightened awareness of sin. To avoid this enemy's influence over our life, we must be surrendered to God wholeheartedly, cease from our self-effort, be humble and honest in purpose, and have a hatred of sin. Only when we see by His grace how united we are with Him in His death and resurrection will we be equipped to fight an aggressive war against our natural inclinations—and against the evil one.

For the gospel "is veiled to those who are perishing, whose minds the god of this age has blinded" (2 Corinthians 4:23). "The whole world lies under the sway of the wicked one" (1 John 5:19). We're instructed to not be "handling the word of God deceitfully" (2 Corinthians 4:2). Satan will do that, and he has been able to change and dilute the message of the cross not only to individuals but in the church as well. Many cities today display great and beautiful churches with a cross on its highest peak, but sadly the participants may be far from God's intended purpose, and Christianity becomes a mockery instead of a glory to God.

Listen to the words of the nineteenth-century Welsh speaker and author Jessie Penn-Lewis:

> A messenger of the cross once drove along a street in one such city, and while gazing at the innumerable crosses standing out against the brilliant blue sky, there suddenly rang out in his ears a hideous satanic laugh, indescribably mocking, as the evil one cried, "I have taken the symbol of conquest, and used it against my Conqueror." Under the "sign of

the cross," multitudes can be under the sway, and in the power of the archenemy of God. (from *The Warfare with Satan*)

With so much deception in the world, we need to be conscientious followers of the Lord, aware of the dangers before us as we accept His invitation: "Learn from Me, for I am gentle and lowly in heart, and you will find rest for your souls" (Matthew 11:29).

CHAPTER 10

CHOSEN OF GOD

We can know God only as He reveals Himself to us. Mere intellectual knowledge of Him will not transform our soul or bring true knowledge of God. It is as the apostle Paul stated: "When it pleased God, [He] separated me from my mother's womb and called me through His grace, to reveal His Son in me" (Galatians 1:15-16). Every sincere and holy thought we ever had about God—even as a child—was cultivated in our hearts and minds by God. It had to happen by grace. Without that grace, "there is none who seeks after God" (Romans 3:11).

Paul also says, *He chose us in Him* before the foundation of the world, that we should be holy and without blame before Him in love, having predestined us to adoption as sons by Jesus Christ to Himself" (Ephesians 1:45). His choosing us in Christ means that He chose us not because of something good He saw in us, for "there is none righteous, no not one; there is none who understands; there is none who seeks after God" (Romans 3:10-11). Rather, He chose us because He willed to choose us for the glory of Himself and the glory of His Son. This choosing is something we can't explain; we can only come to the realization of how truly destitute we are, and how privileged we are when He chooses us.

To think we can do something to gain His favor or please Him will lead us on a meandering frustrating path. Unless God gives us eyes to see and the drawing power in our life to pursue Him, we could never come to Him for anything. Once we see our depraved condition, and our incapacity to redeem ourselves and accept the sacrifice Christ made for our sins, we can move forward in our spiritual journey with Him.

God not only wants us forgiven of our sins, but requires us to leave our old life behind and enter the new life He has for us. God chose us and pursues us so we can fully comprehend this. This is His goal for us:

> He chose us in Him before the foundation of the world, that we should be holy and without blame before Him in love, having predestined us to adoption as sons by Jesus Christ to Himself, according to the *good pleasure of His will*, to the *praise of the glory of His grace*, by which He made us accepted in the Beloved. (Ephesians 1:4-6)

Just as He brought salvation into our lives, His desire is to make us holy and without blame before Him in love for His pleasure and glory.

"The Spirit Himself bears witness with our spirit that we are children of God" (Romans 8:16). God wants sons and daughters to be brought into His family. Adopted children do not choose their own father or mother, but are chosen by their adoptive parents. Their adoption is approved by a committee or judge, and a legal transaction takes place. It's similar with our adoption as children of God. We're chosen by God the Father and come to Him through Jesus Christ. As adoptive children entering His family, we need to know and accept what has been given us. We should no longer feel insecure and hopeless in our depraved condition, but accept His "love, joy, peace, longsuffering, kindness, goodness, faithfulness, self-control" (Galatians 5:22). God secures us into His family by His Spirit for time and eternity.

As we're brought into our new home, we should know that our Father hates sin, and we need a change to take place in our life by His grace. By accepting our crucified position—that when He died, we died out to our old life and came into a new life (Romans 6:67)—we allow His life to be manifested in and through us. Reckoning as dead the old man within us, we're no longer slaves to sin and self (Romans 6:11-12).

The presence of the Holy Spirit within us confirms this reality and gives us the power to overcome sin and to be witnesses of this great work God does in our lives. Christ has now infused His life into us by His Spirit. What He has worked into us, we then work out with godly "fear and trembling, for it is God who works in you both to will and to do for His good pleasure" (Philippians 2:12-13).

Keeping in mind that it was the blood of Christ that cleanses us from sins, we come to know also "that our old man was crucified with Him, that the body of sin might be done away with, that we should no longer be slaves to sin" (Romans 6:6). It may take some time to realize the full impact of this transaction, but the key in our understanding is to realize that it's all done by grace: "For by grace are you saved through faith; and that not of yourselves: it is a gift of God: not by works, lest any man should boast" (Ephesians 2:89 kjv). There's no aspect of our salvation and cleansing that we can work for or take credit for.

"It pleased God, who separated me from my mother's womb, and called me by his grace, to reveal his Son in me" (Galatians 1:15-16 kjv). There's no other way besides divine revelation of Himself that we come to Him. You may diligently study the Scriptures, and have a theoretical and theological knowledge of Christ, but only when the Spirit of God does a transforming work will we know Him (1 John 5:20).

Peter declared to Jesus, "Thou art the Christ, the Son of the living God" (Matthew 16:16 kjv), and Jesus's response was this: "Blessed art thou, Simon Bar-jona: for flesh and blood hath not revealed it unto thee, but My Father which is in heaven" (Matthew 16:17 kjv).

CHAPTER 11

LORD OF OUR LIFE

In Scripture, Paul points out that since many people did not accept Christ's sacrifice for their sins and denied the warnings of their conscience concerning sin, God would leave them to their depraved natural condition and allow them to continue on their destructive path as an unrepented sinner. "Therefore God gave them up to uncleanness, in the lust of their hearts...who exchanged the truth for a lie.... For this reason God gave them up to vile passions" (Romans 1:24-26).

These were those who openly rejected God's offer of salvation. But then there are others who had their consciences pricked by God to repent of their sin and to repent—but in only a halfhearted way. When God through the Holy Spirit convicts us of sin, it's not only repentance He wants, but a complete surrender of our rebellious selves.

The Jews did not recognize Christ as the only acceptable sacrifice for their sins. "Israel, pursuing the law of righteousness, has not attained the law of righteousness. Why? Because they did not seek it by faith, but as it were, by the works of the law. For they stumbled at the stumbling stone" (Romans 9:31-32). This stumbling stone is ultimately Christ. They thought they could find favor with God by obeying His law in their own strength, and they stumbled—not realizing they needed power from on high to live a righteous life, since it is all grace.

But let's go on. A certain rich young ruler asked Jesus, "What shall I do to inherit eternal life?" When Jesus answered him, salvation through Christ was not presented. First Jesus mentioned the commandments, and he asked this young man about keeping them. The man replied, "All these things I have kept from my youth." Jesus then told him, "Sell all that you have and distribute to the poor." Jesus wanted to know if the rich young ruler would fully commit his heart to the Lord. "But when he heard this, he became very sorrowful, for he was very rich" (Luke 18:18-23). Did he not answer his own question about inheriting eternal life?

Scripture tells us to "grow in the grace and knowledge of our Lord and Savior Jesus Christ" (2 Peter 3:18). The order in our growth in grace is clear: Lord first, then Savior—not Savior first, then Lord. We all have something that's precious to us that God must touch to reveal what stands between us. The Jews didn't accept Christ as their Savior, because they would not accept His lordship, His ownership over them. Instead of surrendering their will to God, they did "what was right in their own eyes" (Judges 21:25), and as a result, Jesus says to them, "The kingdom will be taken from you and given to a nation bearing the fruits of it" (Matthew 21:43). Therefore Paul says, "Blindness in part has happened to Israel until the fullness of the Gentiles has come in" (Romans 11:25).

Unless our stubborn heart and will are broken, we'll never be acceptable in God's sight, never truly able to receive Him as Savior. No one wants to go to hell, and many are convinced that Christ is their way to heaven. They think that by making a profession of faith in Christ, they avoid the wrath to come. For doesn't the Bible say, "For God so loved the world that He gave His only begotten Son, that whoever believes in Him should not perish but have everlasting life" (John 3:16)? From this verse it appears that believing in Christ is our safe passage to heaven.

But before that, we read these words of Jesus: "Unless one is born again, he cannot see the kingdom of God" (John 3:3). So which is it? Or is it both?

Those two passages can be explained in this way. The Holy Spirit brings a person to the point where he'll see the lordship of the Father, and then see his desperate condition, and come to Christ for forgiveness, making a full commitment of the heart to follow Christ. This will result in a "born again" conversion experience. The rich young ruler did not come to that point.

Jesus said to the Pharisees, "You will seek Me, and where I am you cannot come" (John 7:34). Later He says again to them, "I am going away, and you will seek Me, and will die in your sin. Where I go you cannot come" (John 8:21). Why can they not come to where He's going? These religious leaders couldn't follow Him because they hadn't sought God in the way He wanted. It didn't matter how good a life they were living, since "all our righteousnesses are like filthy rags" (Isaiah 64:6).

Jesus speaks about His Father to these Pharisees:

> You have neither heard His voice at any time, nor seen His form. But you do not have His word abiding in you, because whom He sent, Him you do not believe. You search the Scriptures, for in them you think you have eternal life; and these are they which testify of Me. But you are not willing to come to Me that you may have life. (John 5:37-40)

They were blind to the truth because of what their natural mind and understanding told them was right, but their conclusions were mistaken, even though they read the Scriptures. What they first needed was to be humbled, to recognize His lordship, and then to receive Christ's sacrifice for their sins. They believed Abraham was their father (John 8:39), but Jesus told them otherwise: "You are of your father the devil" (John 8:44)—which is one reason they set out to kill Him (John 8:40).

Unless the Spirit of God reveals truth to us, it remains indiscernible. Without light from God, we all are in spiritual darkness. To Nicodemus—a Pharisee and religious ruler of the Jews—Jesus said, "Except a man be born again, he cannot *see* the kingdom of God" (John 3:3 kjv). The problem is that "men loved darkness rather than light" (John 3:19), so unless God gives light, we find ourselves among those "for whom is reserved the blackness of darkness forever" (Jude 13).

To a blind man He healed, Jesus said, "For judgment I have come into this world, that those who do not see may see, and those who see may be blind" (John 9:39). The Pharisees heard this and asked Him, "Are we blind also?" (John 9:40) Jesus explains why He could see what the prideful Pharisees could not: "We speak what We know and testify what We have seen, and you do not receive Our witness" (John 3:11). When Jesus speaks of "We," He means the Father, Son, and Holy Spirit. The Pharisees couldn't see this, because they thought they were in control, and they wouldn't turn over that control to the Lord. Therefore God did not allow them to see.

There may be many today who think they've come to Christ, to the throne of grace—but this may not in fact be so, for their prideful mind may have distorted the truth. In order for us not to get a mindset like many in the past who made such tragic mistakes, let us keep in mind 2 Corinthians 13:5: "Examine yourselves as to whether you are in the faith."

Listen to these words from twentieth-century Bible teacher and author A. W. Pink:

> It is almost unfathomable to realize that there is now in hell multitudes of people who had a deep conviction of sin while they lived here on earth. Their awakened consciences made them aware of their rebellion against their creator and the helplessness of their situation. They had knowledge of the justice of God and the reality that without repentance, everlasting punishment was their fate. Though they experienced such convictions, they became more zealous to flee the wrath of hell, and use Christ and religion as a fire-escape rather than to surrender their hearts completely to the Lord. It was more about self-preservation, and when they were told by some religious leader that "receiving Christ as your personal Savior" was all that was needed to go to heaven, they jumped at the chance. (from *The Holy Spirit*)

The warning here is that we need to make sure we haven't come to Him with only halfhearted repentance and religiosity as a means of avoiding eternal punishment. There's a form of repentance that comes about because of self-preservation. This explains why some professing Christians have such hard hearts. The heart of a false convert hardens itself to the things of God, while God softens the heart of a true convert who'll be open to His Word and His leading.

We can follow our own way of thinking, have a religious leader tell us we're secure, attend many religious services, attempt to keep the Ten Commandments, pray by rote, observe religious holidays, make sacrifices, fast, and even diligently read the Bible—but without making Him Lord of our life with true repentance, all our efforts are in vain.

> For You do not desire sacrifice, or else I would give it; You do not delight in burnt offering. The sacrifices of God are a broken spirit, a broken and contrite heart—These, O God, You will not despise. (Psalm 51:16-17)

Without realizing this truth, we may continue to think we're right in our own eyes (Judges 21:25), even when we're far from right. To keep us in darkness, Satan will continue to blind us, not wanting to lose any of his own. For he "hath blinded the minds of them who believe not" (2 Corinthians 4:4 kjv).

CHAPTER 12

OUR DEPRAVITY

A false conversion puts one on a path of powerlessness, destruction, and a fooling of ourselves. We claim to be a Christian but are unable to live the Christian life God intended. It takes more than just our resolve to come to Christ and be delivered from ourselves; the transformation needs to be initiated and performed by God.

The problem is not so much the sins we commit, but our sinful nature which is the source of our problem. We need victory over our inherently and naturally corrupt self-life and mind. There should come a point in our life where this happens:

> Put off, concerning your former conduct, the old man which grows corrupt according to deceitful lusts, and be renewed in the spirit of your mind, and... put on the new man which was created according to God, in true righteousness and holiness. (Ephesians 4:22-24)

We need a conversion that liberates our soul from the dominion of our sinful nature and frees our mind, emotions, and will to serve and worship God. This may seem very basic, but many in the past went wrong because they didn't understand the basics. Knowing the extent of our depravity sheds light on why we're the way we are.

Here the helpful words of A. W. Pink:

If man was not totally depraved there would be no reason to be made a "new creature in Christ" (2 Corinthians 5:17). Man is so sinful and corrupt He does not have the heart or will to change his disposition. If this were not so he would submit to God's commands without any supernatural operation of the Spirit. We being so corrupt have no desire to seek after God (Romans 3:11) but it is even worse, we are actually filled with enmity against Him (Romans 8:7). Our state before deliverance was being "dead in trespasses and sins" (Ephesians 2:1).

"But as many as received Him, to them He gave the right to become children of God, to those who believe in His name: who were born, not of blood, nor of the will of the flesh, nor of the will of man, but of God" (John 1:12-13). This explains why fallen man ever comes to Christ. It is not because of a will of the flesh, or the will of man, or a persuasion of a preacher or Christian worker but it is the will of God. "If all the angels and saints in heaven and all the godly on earth should join their wills and endeavors and unitedly exert all their powers to regenerate one sinner, they could not effect it; yea, they could do nothing toward it. It is an effect *infinitely* beyond the reach of finite wisdom and power: 1 Corinthians 3:6, 7" (S. Hopkins).

In regeneration the Holy Spirit is the sole agent, and the elected individual does not act but is acted upon. Sorrow for sin, faith in Christ, and a love for God are all superseded by the work of the Holy Spirit in ones life. The regenerated believer now has a new heart, a new disposition, a renovated mind, elevated affections and emancipated will to free him from the bondage of sin. "So then it is not of him who wills, nor of him who runs, but of God who shows mercy" (Romans 9:16). (paraphrased from *The Holy Spirit* by A. W. Pink)

Can you now see better why some who called themselves Christians acted as they did? They never had a transformed life, and they tried living the Christian life in their depraved condition.

The new birth occurs because we are acted upon, the Holy Spirit being the force to make us see. We must make Him Lord of our life, repent of our sins, and totally rely on him to be delivered.

On our own, we would never be convicted of sin within ourselves, for "the heart is deceitful above all things" (Jeremiah 17:9). Nor could we ever be delivered from the bondage of sin without Him. It's all grace— "lest any man should boast" (Ephesians 2:9 kjv). To quote A. W. Pink, "the same person who *invites* us to believe (Isaiah 45:22) also *commands* us to believe (1 John 3:23), and He must also give us the faith to believe (Ephesians 6:23)." And the same person who gave us the faith to believe gives us the strength to resist temptation in our old life.

We're now something new. "We are His workmanship created in Christ Jesus for good works, which God prepared beforehand that we should walk in them" (Ephesians 2:10).

Before we see and experience His grace, we must see how deplorable we are, and how incapable we are to meet His holy requirements. Before we live by His grace, we must see our insufficiency and condemnation. We must experience what Paul did when he said, "O wretched man that I am! Who will deliver me from this body of death? I thank God—through Jesus Christ our Lord!" (Romans 7:24)

CHAPTER 13

TOTAL COMMITMENT

Our role is not to resist the Holy Spirit's promptings, but to allow Him to do a work in our life. As Paul says: "I beseech you therefore, brethren, by the mercies of God, that you present your bodies a living sacrifice, holy, acceptable to God, which is your reasonable service" (Romans 12:1). Christ has given His all to us, and He expects us to give our all to Him. He said this to His disciples: "If anyone desires to come after Me, let him deny himself, and take up his cross, and follow Me. For whoever desires to save his life will lose it, but whoever loses his life for My sake will find it" (Matthew 16:24-25). You should be either committed to follow Him or not.

The church at Laodicea was lukewarm, caught between the things of this world and giving their all over to Him. They were neither hot nor cold about the things of God, and the Lord expressed His feelings toward them by saying: "I will vomit you out of My mouth" (Revelation 3:16). God knows what is in man, with each person's "self" at the center. So we need to surrender that self-life to Him.

Jessie Penn-Lewis gives more insight into the total surrendering of His chosen ones:

> Meanwhile the attacks of the adversary upon the redeemed, are turned by the all-wise Lord into the training and fitting of them, for their great destiny in the coming reign of the Conqueror. The Victor

of Calvary calls into one life with Himself all who accept His redemption, His cross, His kingship, and complete control. In the wondrous purpose of the grace of God, He determined to create through the death on Calvary a new race in the likeness of His Son, Who would be the "first-born among many brethren" (Romans 8:29)—a new race which will reign with Him, and in the fullness of time take the place of Satan and his angels in the government of the earth.

The Adversary knows he has lost one of his subjects, but that he will never cause much other loss to his kingdom if he can but retain some hold of him, and prevent him *entirely* escaping from his power. To this end *He seeks to keep back the soul from full surrender to God.*

"Ananias, why hath *Satan* filled thy heart to deceive the Holy Ghost, and to keep back part..." (Acts 5:3, m.).

It was at a time when all were placing themselves and their possessions entirely at the disposal of the Lord, that Ananias looked on. He possibly did not want to be singular, so not realizing the character of the God he was trifling with, he laid part of his possessions at the Apostles' feet, pretending that it was "all"! Peter filled with the Spirit, discerned the truth, and his stern words at once unveil the source of the sin! *Satan* had "filled his heart" to make him "keep back part." It would have been better not to have offered at all, for God only desires voluntary surrender, and absolute honesty of purpose toward Himself. (from *The Warfare with Satan*)

Maybe some of those misguided groups we discussed earlier were trying to be committed to both Christ and the world. They may have believed Satan's lies and held back something for themselves. God says we're to come out from among them, for He will not be mocked or trifled with by those who want to straddle the fence and have their loyalty divided. Nothing should be held back—keeping in mind what a disastrous end it was for Ananias and Sapphira, his wife (Acts 5:1-11).

A good example of commitment to God for His chosen ones can be seen in the relationship between a man and a woman. When one pursues a mate in life, what is the most important element before making the final choice of marriage? Do you choose the other person because you have the same interests and enjoy doing the same things. Is it having a similar mind concerning the issues and philosophies of life? Is it just being infatuated with one other? Or is it a combination of all these?

Those reasons are all elements of what is needed for becoming marriage partners, but what really needs to happen to make this a lasting relationship is to take a "leap of faith" and give one's heart completely over to the other. As time goes on, interests differ, interpretation of Scripture may differ, political views may change, our physical appearance changes, and dry times will come, but it will be a heart committed to one another that will keep the relationship intact.

What is it that you really want from your partner in life? Isn't it mostly a heart totally committed to you? What happens when one gives their all and the other doesn't? The committed partner feels slighted and insecure.

Is this not what God wants from us—a heart totally committed to Him? Any other type of worship of Him is basically useless. If our hearts aren't totally committed to God, how is God affected? That's hard to say, but we saw God's reaction to Ananias and Sapphira (Acts 5:5-11), and toward the wilderness wanderers after they worshiped the golden calf (Exodus 32:7-10). God tells us: "Draw near to God and He will draw near to you" (James 4:8).

When Christ died for us, He gave His all, and we need to do the same for Him. With Christ giving His all, when we likewise give our all, the barriers are taken down between us for a deep and personal relationship to occur. Without it, no close relationship occurs—no real walk with the One who has come into our life. God can get from us sacrifices, praises, money, etc., but unless we can totally surrender ourselves to Him, we fall short of what He wants from us.

If we have a good relationship with our spouse and Lord, what could deteriorate each relationship? There are many things that could, but lying, mistrust, and infidelity are near the top of the list. They're the opposite of truth, trust, and commitment.

"No one can serve two masters; for either he will hate the one and love the other, or else he will be loyal to the one and despise the other. You cannot serve God and mammon" (Matthew 6:24). One of our problems is that we think we can serve two masters—the world and God, someone on earth and God. Or we just don't completely let go of doing whatever we want.

We need to give our entire selves over to the Lord. We can then approach Him with the boldness and confidence talked about in these words:

> Therefore, brethren, having boldness to enter the Holiest by the blood of Jesus, by a new and living way which He consecrated for us, through the veil, that is, His flesh, and having a High Priest over the house of God, let us draw near with a true heart in full assurance of faith, having our hearts sprinkled from an evil conscience and our bodies washed with pure water (Hebrews 10:19-22).

CHAPTER 14

THE TRIAL OF OUR FAITH

We need to be careful not to be misinformed or distracted, and not to share our heart with something else other than God. God is testing us in order to reveal the trueness of our faith, just as Peter speaks of:

> You have been grieved by various trials, that the genuineness of your faith, being much more precious than gold that perishes, though it is tested by fire, may be found to praise, honor, and glory at the revelation of Jesus Christ. (1 Peter 1:7)

Paul was one who had many trials throughout life, yet he stayed focus on the things of God. Paul said, "I press toward the goal for the prize of the upward call of God in Christ Jesus" (Philippians 3:14). He immediately adds these words: "Therefore let us, as many as are mature, have this mind…let us walk by the same rule, let us be of the same mind" (3:15-16). Paul's eyes were fixed on the goal—to secure the prize of the high calling of God. He was a "finisher" for the things of God, and he didn't let the things of the world distract him. In sports, people are sometimes called "finishers," because they can stay focused enough to take home the prize. The wilderness wanderers were *not* finishers because they failed to complete the task set before them—that of entering the promised land. In the Psalms, we find a warning for us not to follow their path:

> Do not harden your hearts, as in the rebellion [of
> those in the wilderness],
> as in the day of trial in the wilderness,
> when your fathers tested Me;
> they tried Me, though they saw My work.
> For forty years I was grieved with that generation,
> and said, "It is a people who go astray in their hearts,
> and they do not know My ways."
> So I swore in My wrath,
> "They shall not enter My rest." (Psalm 95:8-11)

God allows us to be tested, and when we fail, we test the patience of God as the wilderness wanderers did. The message for us is this: "Today, if *you* will hear His voice, do not harden your hearts" (Hebrews 4:7).

Only weeks after God delivered the Israelites from the Egyptians and their slavery there, they were grumbling and wanted to return to Egypt (Exodus 16:13). We as believers will also be put to the test to reveal our heart's desires.

In the commercial world, it's unacceptable and even fraudulent to not test a product before it goes to the marketplace. The consumer needs to be confident the product will hold up to its intended use. God does that with us to see if we'll pass His intended purpose. Here is an imperfect analogy, but one that will help us understand what God is doing: God is the consumer, and we are the product being tested. For we are "bought at a price; therefore glorify God in your body and your spirit, which are God's" (1 Corinthians 6:20).

If a commercial product fails a test because of a particular weakness, it should be modified or strengthened so as not to fail again. Our life needs to be tested and then strengthened by God where we have a weakness. God shores us up in our weakness so that we're able to be strong in Him.

Notice that our defects cannot be straightened out on our own; true change is brought about by the Designer, the Maker, and the Redeemer of our lives, in unison with the Holy Spirit. By His grace, He refines His product daily, always molding us into what He wants us to be.

Have you ever made something you were proud of and wanted to show it off? God is doing this with us, as He did also with Abraham, Moses, Joseph, Job, and others. Listen to what He tells Satan about Job: "Have you considered My servant Job, that there is none like him on the earth, a blameless and upright man, one who fears God and shuns evil?" (Job 1:8)

God is testing us just as He tested those in the wilderness, so that He might prove Himself sufficient in our lives to enter His rest. Theirs was a physical rest; ours is a spiritual rest.

> Therefore, since a promise remains of entering His rest, let us fear lest any of you seem to have come short of it. (Hebrews 4:1)

> For he who has entered His rest has himself also ceased from his works as God did from His. Let us therefore be diligent to enter the rest, lest anyone fall according to the same example of disobedience. (Hebrew 4:10-11)

God was ashamed of the wilderness wanderers, and was so upset He wanted to annihilate them in the wilderness and start anew with Moses. Only Moses was able to stand in the gap and negotiate for them. We as Christians need to see where God is leading and be diligent in our pursuit of entering His rest, with Christ being our intercessor. Jacob "was left alone; and a Man [God] wrestled with him until the breaking of day" (Genesis 32:24). At the break of day, Jacob told this One, "I will not let You go unless You bless me!" (Genesis 32:26).

Paul gives us this instruction: "Work out your own salvation with fear and trembling; for it is God who works in you both to will and to do for His good pleasure" (Philippians 2:12). We're to not let Him go until He completes His work in us. If sickness, injury, or emotional hurt come into our life, learn from it and move closer to God for comfort and strength. He has ordered the trial, and He will get us through it—rest on that fact.

If we fail the test, I'm sure the Lord will give us another opportunity to get it right. The trials we go through will uncover the intentions of our heart, and if you see any fault in yourself, repent.

This is one way God speaks to us. We need to spiritually discern what is from our flesh life. If we have an uncontrolled desire to do something wrong, we need to repent and have Him fix our problem.

Those wayward groups we discussed earlier should have been convicted about what they were doing wrong, and should have come to Him for the solution. If they repented of their wrong, God would give them what they needed to turn from their evil path. Christ not only died for our sin, but wants us to have victory over our self-life. God sends the dissecting knife to discern our thoughts and desires.

> For the word of God is living and powerful, and sharper than any two-edged sword, piercing even to the division of soul and spirit, joints and marrow, and is a discerner of the thoughts and intents of the heart. (Hebrews 4:12)

The sword or knife is brought from God to separate the flesh life from the spiritual life. Many times we don't even know we're doing wrong, and it must be brought to our attention. It may even be something done unconsciously.

Here's an example. There was a group of board members in a large fundamental Christian church who voted to cut expenses on the health plan of their church staff. One thing they cut was maternity benefits. But the board members were older, and their families didn't need maternity benefits; consciously or unconsciously, they cut them out, even though other staff members needed it.

Those so-called Christian slaveholders, as well as those Christians who supported Hitler, needed enlightenment from above, and they needed then to act on that persuasion. We as God's people, have the same selfish motives as unbelievers, and we constantly need to be reminded of our shortfalls. Our old life cannot be corrected; it is totally corrupt. That which is flesh is flesh, and needs to be backfilled by His life. The dissecting knife needs to do its work so we won't be like those who kept following their natural selfish desires and never received the spiritual help God provided.

CHAPTER 15

MOVING FORWARD

Was there ever such a sad story as that of those who walked after the pillar of cloud by day and a flame of fire by night without entering God's promised rest He had for them? What was only a twelve-days journey to the promised land took forty years of fruitless wandering, only to perish in the sand. Those Israelites trusted God's commandment to apply the blood of the lamb to the doorpost, and they trusted Him to walk through the Red Sea on dry ground, but they lacked the mindset and the courage to take the next step and be led into the promised land of rest. They could have saved themselves forty years of wandering in the wilderness by simply taking the next leap of faith in the beginning of their journey.

The wilderness wanderers were in the doldrums, going nowhere in life. For us to not fall into their pattern of life, "Let us therefore be diligent to enter that rest" (Hebrews 4:11). There may be some decision that needs to be made that the Lord is pressing on your heart, or a surrendering that needs to be resolved, or a letting go of something that needs to happen.

Therefore— "Today, if you will hear His voice..." (Hebrews 4:7)—today, step out and cross that Jordan, no matter the cost. We need to experience what it means to be delivered from ourselves and to rely on Christ's power to conquer whatever He has set before us.

Joshua's plea to the next generation of Israelites he was leading into the promised land was to make a clear choice. They responded by saying, "We also will serve the Lord, for He is our God" (Joshua 24:18). But Joshua wasn't totally taken in by their pious promises and devoted declarations, and he warned them of any hypocrisy in the next verse: "You cannot serve the Lord, for He is a holy God. He is a jealous God; He will not forgive your transgressions nor your sins" (Joshua 24:19). In other words, many were just giving God lip service, without any total commitment behind their words.

People are not to make only a casual commitment to God, and maybe switch their affections to something else in the future. They need to seriously consider the person to whom they're committing themselves: He is "a holy God; He is a jealous God" (Joshua 24:19).

Paul the apostle saw the problem, the struggle—the old nature striving against the new. He stated, "For the good I will do, I do not do; for the evil I will not to do, that I practice" (Romans 7:19). Paul realized that his life was flawed with internal corruption. His life needed to be transformed and conquered by the One who forgave him for his sins. Paul saw that he needed not only to be forgiven of his sins but also to be delivered from the power of his old life, in order to have a life of fellowship with God. He needed and wanted a relationship that was no longer servile but an energizing force that gave him rest from his own doings. Paul did not complain about what life threw at him, but he set his eyes forward on what God was going to do through him—a much different attitude than what was seen among those who wandered in the wilderness for forty years.

Sin separates us from God, and although our sins have been forgiven, we still sin. Our fellowship with God will be greatly curtailed if there is habitual sin or an unresolved issue with a particular sin in our life. For example, David of the Old Testament had a close relationship with God until a sin he committed got between him and God. The sin was bad, and things got worse because the sin wasn't dealt with.

It's the same with all the groups we've talked about so far— they needed to be transparent to themselves, just as they were already transparent to God. God will not tolerate certain things in our life. What they needed was to be delivered from whatever was standing in their way between God and them in order to bring them back to God.

We cannot straighten up our own life, as the Pharisees tried to do with theirs. God wants to be our heavenly partner, and He has totally committed Himself to make us right by the giving of His Son, who not only died for our sins but also was raised to give us new life together with Him. When we give our all to God, as David eventually did, all barriers are gone between us and God. It is the same for us, Christ's life becomes infused into ours.

Any self-motivated, legalistic way of approaching God will not get us across the Jordan River. "Do not be deceived, God is not mocked, for whatever a man sows, that he will also reap. For he who sows to his flesh will of the flesh reap corruption, but he who sows to the Spirit will of the Spirit reap everlasting life" (Galatians 6:7-8). Our worship of Him must come from the heart, with a humble desire to be taught and corrected by Him. Until we're filled with His Spirit, we won't have strength and victory over all our shortfalls. "For we are His workmanship, created in Christ Jesus for good works, which God prepared beforehand that we should walk in them" (Ephesians 2:10).

CHAPTER 16

THE CONQUEST OF SIN AND SELF

After we're convicted of our sin and come to Christ, we should experience a clear conscience as proof that our sins are forgiven. We should also have an internal confirmation that we'll spend eternity with Him and obtain a new nature—His nature. But the problem is that we still retain our old nature as well, which still has great influence over us.

Even though God has done such a great work for us and in us, we usually still have a tendency to live by our natural life and look out for number one (ourselves) more than anything else. The natural man within us still tends to be independent and self-dependent. If we continue to live in our old self, we worship God as we think He should be worshiped, and many times we're blinded to the true worship of Him. As a result of this dominant old nature, we may lose our heart for God to self, and we never get truly molded into the person God would like us to be. We need to see ourselves as we really are, and we should be open to God to reveal the path to freedom.

Notice how God reveals to the priestly prophet Ezekiel what is going on with those Israelites who worshiped Him wrongly:

> So they come to you as people do, and they hear your words, but they do not do them; for with their mouth they show much love, but their hearts pursue their own gain. (Ezekiel 33:31)

Those Israelites kept up an outward appearance of true worship, but their hearts were pursuing their own selfish motives. Their worship was for their own self-glory, self-comfort, self-pleasure, and self-preservation. There are times when we too can get caught up in the self-life.

To some extent, we're still under bondage to self and sin, no matter how spiritual we think we are. Even after having our sins forgiven, we still sin and need continual cleansing from our sins, which comes by the same power that cleansed us when we first came to Christ for salvation—by His blood. There's a need to be continually freed from the power of our old sinful self, which vies for power with the new life.

In the following words, Jessie Penn-Lewis explains what we need to know about our new position in Christ to have control and power over our self-life tendencies.

> The sinner and the Savior were one in the sight of God as the Redeemer hung upon His cross. The Apostle says that He bore our sins on the tree, "that *we having died* unto sins might live unto righteousness!" (1 Peter 2:24) It was the sinner who died when the Substitute died! Died in Him to the sins which He bore for him! It could never be that He bore our sins, and died for us, purely that He might forgive us our sins, and leave us still under their power, and hence under the power of Satan! The words of the Apostle make it quite plain that He bore our sins on the tree so that in Him we should die to them—or be delivered from them—and henceforth live a new life "unto righteousness," for by His stripes we are healed from our sin-stricken condition, and set free to live only unto God.
>
> "To this end was the Son of God manifested, that He might destroy the works of the devil" (1 John 3:8). The Adversary holds his captives in his realm by keeping them under the bondage of a guilty conscience over the sins of their past, or the power of present sin. But when the sinner sees that

the Lord bore his sins on the tree, and *took the sinner there also,* the first ground is taken from the devil, for the Spirit takes possession of the redeemed one, and reveals the living Christ dwelling in the heart by faith. "Crucified" is His message to the liberated one— "Crucified with Him...no longer be in bondage to sin." (Romans 6:6)

But is there no fight? Yes—but after the will is surrendered, and kept on the Lord's side in every hour of temptation, it is conflict between the Holy Spirit in His strong desire to conquer the flesh, and the flesh in its innate involuntary resistance to being conquered! The deciding factor is the *will* of the surrendered believer. *"To whom ye yield yourselves,* his servants ye are," writes the apostle Paul to the Romans. If the redeemed one persistently asserts his position as crucified with Christ, and affirms continuously that "they that are of Christ Jesus *have* crucified the flesh," *refusing* at the same time to heed the demands of the flesh, the Holy Spirit brings to bear the victory of Calvary upon the "works of the flesh," and crucifixion with Christ becomes experimentally true. (from *The Warfare with Satan*)

Many of those people in the groups we discussed earlier never realized their need to be freed from themselves and their sin. They became slaves to their own selves. We obtain true freedom when we acknowledge and experience what it means to be "crucified with Him, that the body of sin might be done away with, that we should no longer be slaves to sin" (Romans 6:6). Freedom from our self-life and from the power to sin is needed, and with this in mind let us look at the significance of baptism.

After we enter salvation, we're told to be baptized (Acts 10:47-48). Baptism is a public statement regarding the change and commitment that took place in our lives when we believed in Christ to deliver us. It figuratively identifies us with the death, burial, and resurrection of the Lord Jesus Christ—when Christ died, we died with Him (Romans 6:16). Figuratively our sin and sin nature died in Him, "for he who has died has been freed from sin" (Romans 6:7).

He not only took my sins to the cross; He took me. "I am crucified with Christ...." (Galatians 2:20 kjv). Not only was the sinner's sin laid upon Him, but the person of the sinner as well; we then need to see that when Christ rose from the dead, we rose with Him (Romans 6:5). This is emblematic of what actually took place. After spiritual death, we were delivered from the bondage of sin and self, and given a new heart—a redemptive self, with the right desires to live out our new life. As Paul says, "For if we died with Him, we shall also live with Him" (2 Timothy 2:11). We cannot be resurrected with Him unless we died with Him, and that happened at our conversion, which we may never have realized.

It has all been done for us. We came to Christ because He drew us to Him, and we were delivered from sin and cleansed by His life because He provided the means. It's all grace.

> For if we have been united together in the likeness of His death, certainly we also shall be in the likeness of His resurrection, knowing this, that our old man was crucified with Him, that the body of sin might be done away with, that we should no longer be slaves of sin. For he who has died has been freed from sin. (Romans 6:5-7)

Not realizing the co-death you had with the Savior can keep you a constant slave to self and sin. You may think you're a free person when in actuality you're a slave to your selfish desires, to your passions, and to Satan.

When a person has been delivered from self and sin, they now become bondslaves to Christ (1 Corinthians 7:22). A bondslave of Christ is much different from a bondslave of man. It appears to be a contradiction—being a servant yet free—but as we give control of our lives over to God, He frees us from ourselves, and we obtain true liberty. A bondslave of Christ is forgiven of all his trespasses—past, present, and future. He willfully follows Christ and His teachings because of a desire put within to do so. It is no longer a burden, because he now "goes with the flow" of His life in ours. He no longer follows an outward law; rather, "the life which I now live in the flesh I live by the faith of the Son of God, who loved me and gave himself for me" (Galatians 2:20 kjv).

When we recognize this as a fact and reckon it as true (Romans 6:11), we become free from worry and anxiety, because *He* does not worry and is not anxious. Why should the One within us worry or be anxious, if He is in control of all things?

We're now one with Him, and we're considered in the family of God, as seen in what Paul told the Galatian church:

> For you are all sons of God through faith in Christ Jesus. For as many of you as were baptized into Christ have put on Christ. There is neither Jew nor Greek, there is neither slave nor free, there is neither male nor female; for you are all one in Christ Jesus. And if you are Christ's, then you are Abraham's seed, and heirs according to the promise. (Galatians 3:26-29)

We're now one with Christ because we have His life dwelling within us. True worship is no longer serving self or doing something to please God, but serving Him with a new heart and a capacity to love Him as well as others.

As Christians, we shouldn't be in a weak position trying to control ourselves or fight temptation in our life. When trials come, we need only to consider the accomplished fact that we are "dead indeed to sin, but alive to God" (Romans 6:11). We're delivered from the power of sin, "for sin shall not have dominion over you" (Romans 6:14).

We shouldn't dwell on the fact that even now, or in the past, we've had little success overcoming the self-life and temptation. We must believe what God says in His Word: "If we have been united together in the likeness of His death, certainly we also shall be in the likeness of His resurrection" (Romans 6:5). If God says in His Word that you have been crucified and risen with Him, believe it. Make it a fact in your life.

Even though there may be a continued defeat, there should come a point in your life when you realize and experience the victory. Don't try to crucify yourself; He Himself has accomplished the crucifixion; it is grace, and we only have to acknowledge that we were "crucified with Him." We no longer try to fight temptation with our old life, but rest in Him—His life in ours—to do the fighting. Our mind needs to reject the temptation of fighting this ourselves, and to realize that the Person who won the battle over sin and Satan will fight the battle for us. Again, "Likewise you also reckon yourselves to be dead indeed unto sin" (Romans 6:11). We need to make this fact good in our experience, to count on it and rely on it.

God doesn't alter the life we obtained naturally from our parents, but has given us a *new* spiritual life which is born of God. He doesn't try to educate our natural life, or simply have us improve our natural life; rather, He imparts *new* life. The old life in the believer is as corrupt as that in the non-believer. How ridiculous it is for us to pray to the Lord to make us good and loving, when what we obtained at conversion was His good and loving life. When our old passions and temptations come, we need to remember what He has done, and not rely on our natural strength to overcome those passions and lusts which overcame us in the past.

Guided by the Holy Spirit, emotions can be funneled in the right direction and used by Him for His glory. His Spirit is the One now directing our spirit; it's no longer the self-life in control. Before, we "walked according to the course of this world, according to the prince of the power of the air" (Ephesians 2:2); now we "walk in newness of life" (Romans 6:4).

"Therefore brethren, we are debtors—not to the flesh, to live according to the flesh. For if you live according to the flesh you will die; but if by the Spirit you put to death the deeds of the body, you will live." (Romans 8:12-13)

Again, "Do not be deceived, God is not mocked; for whatever a man sows, that he will also reap. For he who sows to his flesh will of the flesh reap corruption, but he who sows to the Spirit will of the Spirit reap everlasting life" (Galatians 6:7-8).

CHAPTER 17

CIRCUMCISION OF THE FLESH

When we were redeemed, we were given a new heart with new desires. Our old heart should have been removed from its place of supremacy—that part of us that wants to do the controlling and has a tendency to sin. With this new heart, we know the direction we should be going, and we should realize that our fleshly life won't take us there.

The Pharisees couldn't grasp this concept. Keep in mind that it's no longer a matter of an outward display of our religion (like that of the Pharisees), but of an inward reality and certainty that we are the children of God. We are now the "circumcision," having been circumcised "without hands" (Colossians 2:11 kjv), as Jessie Penn-Lewis describes:

> "In Him you were circumcised," writes the apostle, "with a circumcision not made by hands" (Colossians 2:11). As if to say, "The knife power of the death of Christ has been applied to you by God, who alone can perform this operation, 'even the offcasting of the whole body of the flesh....'"
> "The casting off, not (as in outward circumcision) of a part, but the whole body of the flesh, the whole carnal nature."
>
> Here we have the application to the sinner of the power of the cross, in a "circumcision not made with hands," actually said to *have* been carried out.

"They who are *of Christ*—made a new creation by Him, so that they are now of Him, and not of the 'first Adam'—*have* crucified the flesh...." The apostle speaks of just as real a circumcision as the Jewish rite, but carried out by no human hands. He speaks too of the "casting off" of not a *part* of the flesh as in circumcision, but of the whole carnal nature. Not a partial work, but a full one. Not a "gradual" mastery of the sins of the flesh, but a casting off of the old Adam life as decisively as the cutting work. (from *All Things New*)

As stated, circumcision is "not a gradual mastery of the sins of the flesh" but a "cutting work" by God. In other words, God doesn't work with you to gradually give you Christ's righteousness; instead, we instantaneously have Christ's righteousness—His "love, joy, peace, longsuffering, gentleness, faith, meekness, self-control" (Galatians 5:22-23 kjv). We received this at salvation when He delivered us from our sins, even though we may not have realized it. It isn't received in small amounts as God is pleased with our performance; rather, it's given in one instance of time.

Paul tells us to "put off" the things of our old nature: "wrath, malice, blasphemy, filthy language," and to "put on the new man who is renewed in knowledge" (Colossians 3:8, 10).

The Jews of the Old Testament had the blood of the animal sacrifices to cover their sins, and they were told to obey the commandments, which was how God expected the Israelites to live. They were in a difficult position—having a covering for their sins only until the Messiah would come, and not having Christ's nature to carry out the commandments. We who live now in an age of grace are very privileged by having been given a new heart, as promised by God by the Old Testament prophet Ezekiel:

Moreover the word of the Lord came to me, saying: "Son of man, when the house of Israel dwelt in their own land, they defiled it by their own ways and deeds.... Therefore I poured out My fury on them.... But I had concern for My holy name, which

> the house of Israel had profaned among the nations wherever they went.... I do not do this for your sake, O house of Israel, but for My holy name's sake.... I will give you a new heart and put a new spirit within you; I will take the heart out of your flesh and give you a heart of flesh. I will put My Spirit within you and cause you to walk in My statues, and you will keep My judgments and do them." (Ezekiel 36:16-27)

With that privilege comes responsibility, as seen from a quote in the book of Hebrews.

> Anyone who has rejected Moses' law dies without mercy on the testimony of two or three witnesses. Of how much worse punishment, do you suppose, will he be thought worthy who has trampled the Son of God underfoot, counted the blood of the covenant by which he was sanctified a common thing, and *insulted the Spirit of grace*? (Hebrews 10:28-29)

We cannot afford to insult "the Spirit of grace" and make a mockery of what God has given us. It's important to see who we are, who God is, and what God has given us in order to have a continual and fruitful walk with the Savior.

"Where there is no vision the people perish" (Proverbs 29:18 kjv). The prophets of the Old Testament were given visions for insight into the present and the future. These visions were passed on to the people, but in many instances they went unheeded. The Israelites in the wilderness perished because they couldn't see and act upon where God was leading them. A clear vision gives us insight into what we've been given and how we should live. For us to miss what God has given us would be just another tragedy in Christian history.

CHAPTER 18

OUR EMOTIONS

Our emotions can be stimulated in various ways, resulting in various reactions such as love or hate. People, events, and internal desires, can drive us into an emotional frenzy if we let it, as we all have experienced to some degree.

When emotional feelings and religion meet, there are a variety of reactions. Some express themselves boldly in their love for God and even for their salvation, but the source of their love and assurance may be in question. It may be more emotional than a true conversion experience. Simply feeling affections toward God does not assure our salvation. Didn't the Pharisees think they were so right that they thanked God they weren't like other men? They didn't realize they were actually blind, deceived, and boastful in their thoughts.

Then there are those who have visions and hear voices, thinking God is embracing them in a very personal way, and they have a sense that God has redeemed them. Keep in mind that if you have a vision or hear a voice, or even hear a Scripture being quoted, this isn't necessarily from God, for Satan can offer up all these things, including quoting Scripture (Matthew 4:5-6).

Many religious groups have taken their emotional fervor to an extreme. Even the apostle Paul, as a Jewish zealot before his conversion, persecuted Christians, thinking he was doing God a service. Satan was behind his emotional zeal and enthusiasm to do evil.

Religious passion, visions, and voices may excite our emotions, but only a sober-minded approach, built on principles according to God's Word, can secure our place in heaven.

The colonial American pastor and theologian Jonathan Edwards writes,

> Many believe the Holy Spirit is their inner voice not only to guide but to tell them they are loved, forgiven, elect, and so forth. How many false emotions have arisen from this delusion! I fear there are many who have gone to hell because they were deceived by it. (as paraphrased from *Treatise on Religious Affections*)

When a person is truly redeemed by the blood of Christ, the Holy Spirit lives in their heart to bring them closer to God. The Holy Spirits gives us the confidence, the will, and the ability to be holy and to pursue Him. "Being confident of this very thing, that He who has begun a good work in you will complete it" (Philippians 1:6). When our feelings and emotions align with His purpose, we begin to grow in the way He wants us to.

A very emotional mind that isn't under the Holy Spirit's control will think in a simplified way: What *feels* right in my mind *is* right. Actions that come from an emotional mind carry a strong sense of certainty, but the conviction that you're right may not always be correct—as seen from the examples of some of the professed believers in the past that we spoke of. A rational mind uses more of their intelligence and reason to come to conclusions, but they also can be greatly influenced by emotions. As someone has said, "All decisions are made from emotions, and then are later justified by intelligence and reason."

We all have emotions which can guide how we think, feel, and behave. Fear is an emotion that can overcome even the strongest parts of our intelligence.

The wilderness wanderers in the Old Testament are a good example of this. They wouldn't go into the promised land because they feared the giants in the land.

Emotions are far more powerful than thoughts, and can even overcome our rational way of thinking. Look at the many rebellions in the world that happened quickly because an emotional crowd rebelled without thinking of the consequences. Many put away their democratic government in a short period of time because someone persuaded them they could do a better job to lead the country. You may have seen old newsreels showing the emotional crowds supporting Franco in Spain, Mussolini in Italy, and Hitler in Germany. There are many other examples of how emotional fury has changed history, including that of the crowd in Jerusalem asking Pontius Pilate to release the criminal Barabbas and to crucify Jesus, who had done no wrong.

The so-called Christian slaveholders of the American South may have feared the black man would someday become their equal, so they held down the blacks physically and emotionally. The professed German Christians feared where their country was heading and reacted in a way that was unthinkable. They helped Hitler come to power, which allowed him to go ahead with his racial cleansing policy, which in the process slayed millions of Jews. All this came about by supposedly sane, rational-thinking, God-worshiping people who were caught up emotionally.

God's intent after creating the heavens and the earth was to create man. He said: "Let Us make man in Our image, according to Our likeness" (Genesis 1:26). God made man with qualities not found in other creatures, qualities that reflected God's own image. He made man in the "likeness of Him," but only Christ was made in the perfection of Him. Christ is the perfect image of Him, while we are imperfect—especially after the consequences of Adam's sin. God didn't want to interact with robot-like creatures that would respond to His every command; He wanted relationship with those having emotions, who were able to have feelings, and think rationally, and make choices. God wanted to have a volunteer army of individuals who would act together in a deeper sense than His angelic creations, or even than Adam and Eve in their innocent state. God wanted to communicate with people having the ability to feel love, hurt, joy, and compassion.

To get our emotional lives in tune with Him, God sends us trials in which we can learn more about ourselves and how our emotions control our behavior. When Jesus fasted for forty days, Satan was there to try Him in His weakened state (Matthew 4:11), but Jesus would not be diverted from the Father's will for Him. This is in contrast to Adam and Eve, who lived in God's presence in the garden of Eden, without a sin nature, and yet Satan was able to tempt them and have them move away from God:

> So when the woman saw that the tree was good for food, that it was pleasant to the eyes, and a tree desirable to make one wise, she took of its fruit and ate. She also gave to her husband with her, and he ate. (Genesis 3:6)

Before that, the woman said to the serpent,

> We may eat the fruit of the trees of the garden; but of the fruit of the tree which is in the midst of the garden, God has said, "You shall not eat of it, nor shall you touch it, lest you die." (Genesis 3:1-3)

Adam and Eve yielded to their emotional desires, not to what God commanded them to do. If they had everything in life they needed, why eat of the fruit of the forbidden tree? They ate because their desires overwhelmed them. Their desires were stronger than their loyalty to God and His Word. Eve disobeyed God because she wanted that good-looking fruit that could make her wise. Adam ate because of his desire to please Eve. Adam and Eve knew their actions were wrong, but both succumbed to their emotions, and Satan was there to prod them to continue down that path of destruction.

We also can easily make bad choices because of the strong desires and emotions in our life. Imagine a Christian married man who has deep affections for a women other than his wife. He knows it is wrong, but his lustful feelings and passions are screaming out for that other women. He tries to muster up enough will to fight his feelings, but he may lose that fight and become overwhelmed by his desire for the forbidden fruit. How could this be avoided? And how should this man deal with the problem as he slips further away from his God, his wife, and his own integrity?

First of all, he should have been warned and prepared for

something like this before being tempted. He should have realized his crucified position in Christ, in order to have the power to overcome this temptation. Fighting only by our natural self against the temptation could very well lead to failure, as seen many times in the past with many others.

After realizing his desperate situation, he needs to do damage control and plead for God's mercy and grace. If temporarily relieved, he should strive to know God and himself better, so as not to be so vulnerable. We know that Christ "gave Himself for our sins, that He might deliver us from this present evil age" (Galatians 1:4); that needs to be realized, acted upon, and made a reality in all our lives.

Sorrow, pleasure, love, fear, enthusiasm, and curiosity are all part of our life, but when any of these is out of control, it can draw us away from God and back to our own desires and needs. Many of our decisions are made because our emotional tendencies go in a direction which may not be in line with God's leading or His Word. You may justify your actions to yourself and others as Adam and Eve tried to do, only to find yourself in a similar position as Adam and Eve, disobeying God and becoming separated from Him.

We shouldn't become emotionless, but our emotions should be guided and influenced by the Holy Spirit residing in us. A personality with true love, sorrow, and enthusiasm is one that shines from Him.

With our new life in Christ, our affections should be on fire for Him, for our fellow man, and for a controlled self-life. We should also be able to despoil Satan and all his hosts of evil that attack us. We don't live in the garden of Eden, but in a type of spiritual war zone, and therefore we're told,

> Be strong in the Lord and in the power of His might. Put on the armor of God, that you may be able to stand against the wiles of the devil. For we do not wrestle against flesh and blood, but against principalities, against powers, against the rulers of darkness of this age, against spiritual hosts of wickedness in heavenly places. (Ephesians 6:10–12 kjv)

Remember your position in Christ whenever you're tempted, overwhelmed by emotions, or feeling offended, sorry for yourself, guilty, or anxious for unknown reasons. Satan is there to incite us to continue going back to our former self.

More detail on Satan's tactics to drive us away from God and bring us down can be seen from Jessie Penn-Lewis's writings:

> The darts tipped with fire from hell fall upon the believing one, and they are quenched, but let a fiery dart fall, and find the believer *questioning the keeping of God*, then how quickly the sting is felt! Now the "helmet of salvation" is necessary, for the "darts" are generally directed against the head—or the *thoughts*. An evil suggestion is shot in as an arrow to the mind, but the believer must quickly refuse it, and claim "salvation," which is, in other words, the cleansing of the blood which was shed at Calvary. If the thought is not at once rejected, and cleansed, it lies as a poisoned dart, unheeded at the time, later on to produce sad results.
>
> See the prince of darkness following him; note the hosts of wicked spirits watching him! See! Something happens in his path—he is injured, insulted or ignored. Now is the adversary's time! A "fiery dart" is winged—the thought flashes into the mind, "How unfair; how unjust: it is necessary you speak—you must defend yourself for righteousness' sake!" Now is the time to "take the helmet of salvation." Quickly, *quickly* reject the thought, and cry, "The blood of the Lamb cleanses."
>
> But supposing the fiery dart is unheeded. At the moment it is not noticed, but it is there in the mind! It is a spark from hell. The enemy is content to let it lie. He has gained a spot from which he can act later on. Days pass, and the believer meets the one who injured him. A coldness comes over him, circumstances arise, before he is aware he finds himself in friction and resentment. The fiery dart

has done its work, the breastplate of righteousness is gone, and defeat follows. Sorrow, confession, shame, and restoration come next, but what a loss of time! It has been victory for the adversary, and dishonor to the Lord! Yes, the helmet of salvation is needed for the protection of the *thoughts,* and the retaining of the heart in peace. (from *The Warfare with Satan*)

The enemy is there to deceive, tempt, and discourage. One sin can bring us down—as seen in the lives of many, including David, "a man after His own heart" (1 Samuel 13:14). Even after spiritual successes in our life, we have to be on our guard against a prideful position in Christ. Jesus said to the seventy who were sent out,

I saw Satan fall like lightning from heaven. Behold, I give you the authority to trample on serpents and scorpions, and over all the power of the enemy, and nothing shall by any means hurt you. Nevertheless do not rejoice in this, that the spirits are subject to you, but rejoice because your names are written in heaven. (Luke 10:18-20)

When God gives us a clear mind and conscience and power over our self-life and our emotions, rejoice—not because of this new life and power you've received. Rather, with a humble spirit, rejoice because your name is written in heaven. It's most important not to be driven by our emotions, but by our will knowing His will.

CHAPTER 19

A CAUTIOUS WALK

As we discover in Scripture, David—a highly respected figure in the Bible—fell into sin. David was blessed by God, anointed by the prophet Samuel to be Israel's king, and he was mighty in battle. For the most part he was loved by the people. But one day David was tempted and let down his guard. The Bible doesn't gloss over the failures of highly respected figures like David, as we shall see. God was testing David's heart, and those publicized tests were put forth as examples and lessons for us.

The disciples were told by Jesus, "Watch and pray, lest you enter into temptation. The spirit indeed is willing, but the flesh is weak" (Matthew 26:41). As believers we should also know this truth: "The heart is deceitful above all things, and desperately wicked; who can know it? I, the Lord, search the heart, I test the mind" (Jeremiah 17:9-10). We should also embrace the truth for us in this statement from the apostle Paul: "In me (that is, in my flesh) nothing good dwells" (Romans 7:18). We have many things working against us, but with Christ in us, it's inexcusable for us not to have power to deal with any trial, especially since He gave us the promise: "God is faithful, who will not allow you to be tempted beyond what you are able" (1 Corinthians 10:13).

Before David's fall, God blessed him, and his success grew. At one point, David seemed to be overwhelmed with his own success. Maybe he began to be puffed up with pride over what God had done through him. David had killed a lion and a bear, and had slayed Goliath. He heard things like, "Saul has slain his thousands, and David his ten thousands" (1 Samuel 29:5). His natural tendency might have been to think of himself more highly than the One who had lifted him to his position in life. If he was in a prideful mindset, he may not have been aware that he was opening his life for Satan to work, because "pride goes before destruction" (Proverbs 16:18).

David's downfall came while his army was out on the battlefield, and "David tarried still at Jerusalem" (2 Samuel 11:1 kjv). While in his palace—which was probably higher than other buildings nearby—David gazed upon Bathsheba bathing on her rooftop. While gazing, David lusted after her. He then called for her, an encounter ensued, and subsequently she became pregnant. David, not wanting those of his kingdom or the surrounding nations to know what he had done, devised a plan to cover up his sin.

An appropriate phrase for what happened next is: "Oh what a tangled web we weave when we practice to deceive." David ordered Joab, his commander, to put Bathsheba's husband, Uriah, on the frontlines to be killed in battle. And so it happened. This was done to make it appear Bathsheba became pregnant by her husband Uriah before he went to battle.

David may have been successful in hiding his crime from man, but he could never hide it from God, who examines every heart and mind. "There is no creature hidden from His sight, but all things are naked and open to the eyes of Him to whom we must give account" (Hebrews: 4:13).

We can now add murder to his crime of adultery. David's ignoring of his conscience, how he failed to confess and repent of his sin, resulted in his heart becoming hard, and he lost his relationship with God. For those who know God, the consequences of sin are different than they are for those who do not know Him. *Not* knowing God and sinning just adds more offense at the Judgment Day. *Knowing* God and sinning is a serious problem not only for us but for God as well, because of the fact that He cannot deny Himself.

After our salvation, God made His abode in us, as Paul stated: "Christ in you, the hope of glory" (Colossians 1:27). With God being in David's life for time and eternity, He needed to reconcile

David back to Himself to restore that relationship. David was saved by faith, by believing in the Savior who was to come, and therefore he had the same God in Him as we do after we come to Christ for salvation. God cannot tolerate sin in David's life or our life either, so sin has to go. To do that, God's dissecting knife has to do its work.

David's situation—as well as our position as believers—is seen in these words of Paul: "If we believe not, yet He abideth faithful: He cannot deny himself" (2 Timothy 2:13 kjv). Put another way: If we have a living relationship with God, and thus have in us "a friend who sticks closer than a brother" (Proverbs 18:24), and yet we fail Him in some way, He cannot just leave us to ourselves, but must intervene to bring us back.

After Uriah's death, months went by, and David's sin was not revealed until God, the initiator, told Nathan the prophet what David has done. Nathan tactfully approached David by telling him a story of a wealthy man who took a poor man's only sheep for his own. David, thinking the culprit was someone in his kingdom, was appalled at the rich man's behavior and said, "The man who has done this shall surely die!" (2 Samuel 12:5). Nathan responded to David, "You are the man!" (2 Samuel 12:7)—because David had taken Uriah's only wife and added her to his wives.

It was as if a knife was put to David's inner life by Nathan the prophet. When we do wrong, we also need the knife put to our lives, spiritually speaking, in order to cut us open and reveal any wickedness there. Hopefully when we hear His voice, we don't harden our hearts like those "in the rebellion," as mentioned in Hebrews 4:8 about those who fell in the wilderness. God's living and active word is "piercing even to the division of soul and spirit, and of joints and marrow, and is a discerner of the thoughts and intents of the heart" (Hebrews 4:12)—just as it pierced the callous conscience and hardened heart of David.

David's final response to Nathan was deep remorse and a pouring out of his heart toward God. We see this in Psalm 51, which has this heading: "The Psalm of David, when Nathan the prophet came unto him, after he had gone into Bathsheba." This psalm includes these lines:

Have mercy upon me, O God... Cleanse me from
my sin... Create in me a clean heart... Do not take
Your Holy Spirit from me... Restore to me the joy
of Your salvation... Deliver me from the guilt of
bloodshed.... A broken and contrite heart—these,
O God, You will not despise. (Psalm 51:1-17)

If we're a true believer and we sin, we too can find forgiveness
in our time of failure, because we're joined to the Lord as David
was—for "he who is joined to the Lord is one spirit with Him"
(1 Corinthians 6:17).

To understand better this relationship with God, listen to the
opening lines of Psalm 42: "As the deer pants for the water brooks,
so pants my soul for You, O God. My soul thirsts for God, for the
living God." These words are similar to those from the ancient
theologian Augustine: "Thou hast made us for thyself, O Lord,
and our heart is restless until it finds its rest in thee."

CHAPTER 20

PASSIVITY

When we walk with God, we need not only to fight a defensive battle against Satan but to go on the offensive as well. We need to be active participants in this battle, guided by the truth, and not allowing Satan to influence us in any way. Untruth leads to narrow-mindedness, poor spiritual insight, misjudgments, and prejudices, as we've seen in those we studied from the past.

Another important point is that we cannot allow our mind to be tossed around by every thought and feeling that enters it. Our choosing and motivation cannot originate from voices or feelings within, but from biblical truth and the gentle but not compulsive Spirit within. For "the devil walks about like a roaring lion, seeking whom he may devour. Resist him" (1 Peter 5:8-9). Resist what is not truth. Resist any compulsive driving force that isn't from God.

The further from the truth one wanders, the more stiff and rigid their testimony becomes. They become driven by something other than His life within them.

Many of those in the past had a hard and unteachable spirit for this very reason. The Pharisees approach to God is a good example of this. The Pharisees were driven by rules, by what they thought was right, and by their emotions—rather than being led by His Spirit abiding in them. Any deviation from the softness we should have from being in Christ should be brought into question and examined to find the reason for it.

> Watch, stand fast in the faith, be brave, be strong.
> Let all that you do be done with love. (1 Corinthians
> 16:13-14)

Satan sends not only the tares among the wheat—the tares being illegitimate Christians, "sons of the evil one" (Matthew 13:38-39)—but he also sends deceptions (Revelation 12:9) to break up or weaken the wheat. Many honest seekers of God may be deceived and believe things that are just not true. We must be careful in our Christian walk, because we did not possess full knowledge at salvation, and Satan is there to take advantage of us in our ignorance (2 Corinthians 2:11). Making decisions when we don't have full knowledge is dangerous, but not making decisions and allowing a compulsive influence to decide for us is just as dangerous.

Listen to Jessie Penn-Lewis on this:

> The chief condition for the working of evil spirits in a human being, apart from sin, is passivity, the exact opposite to the condition which God requires for His working. Even when there is the surrender of the will to God, with active choice to do His will as it may be revealed, God requires one's cooperation with His Spirit, and the full use of every faculty of the whole man. In short, the powers of darkness aim at obtaining a passive slave, a captive to their will; while God desires a regenerated man who is intelligently and actively both willing and choosing, doing His will in liberation from slavery of spirit, soul and body.
>
> The powers of darkness would make a man a machine, a tool, an automaton; the God of holiness and love desires to make him a free, intelligent sovereign in his own sphere—a thinking, rational, renewed creation created after His own image (Ephesians 4:24). Therefore God never says to any faculty of man, "Be thou idle." (from *War on the Saints*)

Some confuse "surrendering our life to God" with surrendering our minds and will to Him. Passivity submits to any thought that enters our mind without investigating the source of it.

Those groups we mentioned before dishonored God because they could have been driven by their own natural tendencies, interpreted Scripture wrongly, or maybe followed some compulsiveness that wasn't God's leading. It's a warning for us to not be complacent in our walk with God, but to have our minds and will guided by the truth, so we aren't deceived or tossed about by every wind of doctrine.

If we cease to think, reason, and act, believing that God will perform these for us regardless, then we open the door to Satan's working. God's intention is not that we fall into such traps, but that we be proactive and alert, and walk in the light He has provided.

CHAPTER 21

KNOWING GOD

We'll now look at those who allowed God's grace to permeate their lives. They were known by God and knew God intimately. As we read, let us try to understand how God brought about changes in their lives to make them "conformed to the image of His Son" (Romans 8:29). What did they learn that many today have not been able to grasp?

We'll start with Moses of the Old Testament, who was born around 1500 b.c. in Egypt, when the Israelites were enslaved there. While in captivity, the Israelites gained in numbers so much that they became a threat to the Egyptians. To reduce their population, Pharaoh ordered all newborn Israelite males to be thrown into the Nile to drown.

Three months after the birth of Moses, his parents realized they could hide him no longer, so they placed him in a basket hidden in the reeds along the river. When Pharaoh's daughter and her attendants came down to the Nile to bathe, Pharaoh's daughter saw the basket and had one of her attendants retrieve it. They found the baby inside. The sister of Moses stood nearby and suggested to Pharaoh's daughter that they find a woman from the Hebrews to nurse this child. The sister brought back her mother, to whom Pharaoh's daughter said, "Take this child away and nurse him for me, and I will give you your wages" (Exodus 2:9). So the mother had contact with her son Moses at least through the early years of life, and hopefully later in life as well. Moses was brought up in the house of Pharaoh's daughter, and became "learned in all the wisdom of the Egyptians, and was mighty in words and deeds" (Acts 7:22). Another New Testament account gives us a glimpse of what Moses eventually concluded about his situation:

> By faith Moses, when he became of age, refused to called the son of Pharaoh's daughter, choosing rather to suffer affliction with the people of God than to enjoy the passing pleasures of sin, esteeming the reproach of Christ greater riches than the treasures in Egypt; for he looked to the reward. (Hebrews 11:24-26)

Moses "looked to the reward," to the promises made by God to his Israelite forefathers. Those promises can be seen in the book of Genesis, which Moses later wrote, inspired by the Spirit of God. One such promise is found in these words from God to Abraham:

> Know certainly that your descendants will be strangers in a land that is not theirs, and will serve them, and they will afflict them four hundred years. And also the nation whom they serve I will judge; afterward they shall come out with great possessions. (Genesis 15:13-14)

Moses believed God's promise, and had compassion on his fellow Israelites while in Pharoah's household. We're told by Stephen in the book of Acts how Moses put his thoughts and desires into action.

> Now when he [Moses] was forty years old, it came into his heart to visit his brethren, the children of Israel. And seeing one of them suffer wrong, he defended and avenged him who was oppressed, and struck down the Egyptian. For he supposed that his brethren would have understood that God would deliver them by his hand, but they did not understand. And the next day he appeared to two of them as they were fighting, and tried to reconcile

them, saying, "Men, you are brethren; why do you
wrong one another?" But he who did his neighbor
wrong pushed him away, saying, "Who made you
a ruler and a judge over us? Do you want to kill me
as you did the Egyptian yesterday?" Then at this
saying, Moses fled and became a dweller in the land
of Midian, where he had two sons. (Acts 7:23-29)

God says in 1 Corinthians 1:29 "that no flesh should glory in His
presence." So even though it was in the heart of Moses to deliver
the Israelites, God wasn't going to deliver them in the way Moses
thought they should be delivered. Moses wasn't ready for the task,
nor were the Israelites ready to be delivered. Instead, for the next
forty years, Moses would live in a desolate place called Midian,
where God would mold him into the person He wanted him to be.

Keep in mind that it's much the same for us. We can truthfully
acknowledge to God, "You are our Father; we are the clay, and
You our potter; and all we are the work of Your hand" (Isaiah
64:8). When Moses first went to Midian, he was "learned in all the
wisdom of the Egyptians, and was mighty in words and deeds"
(Acts 7:22), but he came out totally different, after living for forty
years in that desolate place. We read in Numbers 12:3, "Now the
man Moses was very humble, more than all men who were on the
face of the earth." The changed Moses who was going to deliver
the Israelites would now be similar to Israel's future deliverer
described in the book of Zechariah: "Behold, your King is coming
to you; He is just and having salvation, lowly and riding on a
donkey" (Zechariah 9:12).

Moses, as a more humble servant of God, was now ready for
the task ahead, which was predetermined before Moses was even
born. We as believers have also been chosen to serve Him in some
way, even before we were born—as seen in these words from Paul:

He chose us in Him before the foundation of
the world, that we should be holy and without
blame before Him in love, having predestined us
to adoption as sons by Jesus Christ to Himself,
according to the good pleasure of His will, to the

praise of His grace, by which He made us accepted in the Beloved. (Ephesians 1:4-6)

Living up to that predetermined plan will be achieved as God works in us to accomplish it.

After Moses spent forty years in Midian, he was tending his flock on the back of the desert when God appeared to him and said,

Behold, the cry of the children of Israel has come to Me, and I have also seen the oppression with which the Egyptians oppress them. Come now, therefore, and I will send you to Pharaoh that you may bring My people, the children of Israel, out of Egypt. (Exodus 4:9-10)

Moses answered, "Who am I that I should go to Pharaoh, and that I should bring the children of Israel out of Egypt?" (Exodus 4:11) This man who once was "learned in all the wisdom of the Egyptians, and was mighty in words and deeds" now shied away from being Israel's deliverer. He had lost his original self-confidence, but was becoming a humble, pliable servant of God, ready to experience what Jessie Penn-Lewis describes:

God was becoming to Moses a greater reality than the things that are seen, and bolder and bolder became his walk of faith, until the unseen grew more real and tangible to him than the visible. How could he fear the "wrath of the king," when he walked in fearless fellowship with the King of kings? (from *Face to Face*)

What a privilege and honor it was for Moses to be taught by God, and to walk in fearless fellowship with Him!

Now let's look at another person whom God transformed. In the New Testament, the man Saul—who would later be known as Paul—was obsessed with keeping the law, and was confident and exuberant in his religious state. He would later describe himself as "a Hebrew of Hebrews; concerning the law, a Pharisee, concerning zeal, persecuting the church; concerning the righteousness which is in the law, blameless" (Philippians 3:56). He had his moral life and Bible doctrine down more than most, but he was living a life completely out of touch with God—until God changed him by His grace.

God met Saul on the Damascus Road. "Suddenly a light shone around him from heaven. Then he fell to the ground, and heard a voice saying to him, 'Saul, Saul, why are you persecuting Me?'" (Acts 9:34). It wasn't what Saul knew about God's Word that opened his eyes, or what he had done for God. Rather, it was what God made known to this man that made the difference. Afterward, he became known as Paul the apostle—quite a turnaround!

We need to see ourselves as we are, and have our eyes opened by God. We must see the truth that Moses and Paul saw—that in ourselves, we cannot please God.

Even after being regenerated, Paul still used his self-knowledge and self-sufficiency to please God until he finally came to an accurate conclusion about himself, as seen in these words:

> For I know that in me (that is, my flesh) nothing good dwells; for to will is present with me, but how to perform what is good I do not find. For the good that I will do, I do not do, but the evil I will not to do, that I practice. (Romans 7:18-19)

Paul goes on to say: "O wretched man that I am! Who will deliver me from this body of death" (Romans 7:24). In the next verse, we're given the solution to that dilemma in Paul's own words: "I thank God—through Jesus Christ our Lord!" (Romans 7:25) When Paul saw how deficient he was in his natural state, his pride, ego, and self-confidence went to shambles.

Another important ingredient in Paul's coming to this conclusion was his honesty with himself and God. He knew he needed God's grace to deliver him from his decrepit and weak condition. Enlightened about his problem, Paul later reveals what he went through in these words:

> I count all things but loss for the excellency of the knowledge of Christ Jesus my Lord: for whom I

have suffered the loss of all things, and do count them but dung, that I may win Christ, and be found in him, *not having my own righteousness*, which is of the law, but that which is *through the faith of Christ*, the righteousness which is of God by faith. That I may know him, and the power of his resurrection, and the fellowship of his sufferings, *being made conformable unto his death*. (Philippians 3:8-10 kjv)

To know Christ and the power of His resurrection—this is achieved not by doing works in ourselves, but by receiving grace to do them. Paul says later to the Philippians, "I press toward the goal for the prize of the upward call of God in Christ Jesus" (Philippians 3:14). The call of God is the same for us: "Let us walk by the same rule, let us be of the same mind" (Philippians 3:16).

God works uniquely in each person to achieve His goal. As we proceed, we'll hear from two others who saw what God wanted them to see about themselves and Him.

Nicholas Herman is one. Born in France in 1611, Nicholas came to the realization that there was no room for striving to please God. He needed to just receive His life, His all and all.

When I was eighteen, I was out for a walk in the woods, trying to think through some problems that had been on my mind for months. All my life I had believed in God and wanted to please him. I had assumed that this was done by deliberate acts of worship, by prayer and study, by discipline and self-control. And I was discouraged because, instead of getting better as I got older, I found myself actually getting worse. The harder I tried, the more I failed.

I was walking along, thinking about these things, when I came to a very beautiful chestnut tree. I'd been watching it all year—the leaves coming fresh and green from the buds, the flowers opening up in early summer.... And now it was loaded with chestnuts. I sat under the tree, and suddenly, like a ray of light bursting in my mind, I got the answer: I was like the tree in winter. Myself, I was nothing—dead, barren, without fruit. And, like the tree, I couldn't change by struggling or sheer effort. I, too, must wait for the hand of my Maker to touch me with life, and change my winter of barren unfruitfulness into first the spring of new life, and then the summer and fall of flower and fruit.

We, too, are dead and barren until God gets hold of our life so that we blossom and bear fruit.

Moving forward in time we see another of the faith, J. C. Ryle, expressing what he possessed in Christ. Born in 1816 in Macclesfield, England, he too came to a similar understanding as Nicholas Herman:

The union between the branch of a vine and the main stem, is the closest that can be conceived. It is the whole secret of the branch's life, strength, vigor, beauty, and fertility. Separate from the parent stem, it has no life of its own. The sap and juice that flow from the stem are the origin and maintaining power of all its leaves, buds, blossoms, and fruit. Cut off from the stem, it must soon wither and die.

The union between Christ and believers is just as close, and just as real. In themselves believers have no life, or strength, or spiritual power. All that they have of vital religion comes from Christ. They are what they are, and feel what they feel, and do what they do, because they draw out of Jesus a continual supply of grace, help, and ability. Joined to the Lord by faith, and united in mysterious union with Him by the Spirit, they stand, and walk, and continue, and run the Christian race. But every jot of good about them is drawn from their spiritual Head, Jesus Christ. (from *Expository Thoughts on John*)

Moses, Paul, Nicholas Herman, and J. C. Ryle each came to realize that they could no longer rely on their natural abilities to please God, but must derive their strength from God, since "no flesh should glory in His presence" (1 Corinthians 1:29). These examples show that when we also come to realize this, we experience what Christ has said: "He who believes in Me, as the Scripture has said, out of his heart will flow rivers of living water" (John 7:38). The living water is His life flowing in ours, His Spirit living in our life.

There's a strong need for us to understand what has transpired in our life in order to give Him room to work. There's a necessity to "present your bodies a living sacrifice, holy, acceptable to God, which is your reasonable service" (Romans 12:1). By totally committing ourselves to having Him fill us with His living water, we can see why our body is called "the temple of the Holy Spirit" (1 Corinthians 6:19). When we empty ourselves of our old life, we give the Holy Spirit room to abide in our life. The Spirit may have resided in us before, but in cramped quarters. When we're free from living life by self, the Holy Spirit now has room to work, giving us His life, strength, and spiritual power, and in particular the ability to commune with Him and know Him better.

Paul compared this relationship to the affections a husband and wife have toward each other, as he proclaimed, "The two shall become one flesh. This is the great mystery, but I speak concerning Christ and the church" (Ephesians 5:31-32). Elsewhere Paul speaks of "the mystery which has been hidden from ages and generations, but now was been revealed to His saints....which is Christ in you, the hope of glory" (Colossians 1:26-27).

We can now be filled with what Christ promised:

> I will pray the Father, and He will give you another Helper, that He may abide with you forever—the Spirit of truth, whom the world cannot receive, because it neither sees Him nor knows Him; but you know Him, for He dwells with you and will be in you. (John 14:16-17)

Since Christ provided the means for us to have this close relationship with Him, let us not fail to experience what Christ has provided.

CHAPTER 22

THE KINGDOM WITHIN

The Jews believed that when their Savior came, He would set up His kingdom on earth and everyone would see that Israel worshiped the true and living God. But it didn't happen that way. Instead of an outward kingdom, Christ came to make a kingdom change *within* His followers. He didn't cast out the rulers of the Jews at the time, but cast out demons and sickness from people. Jesus healed the lame man and told him, "Rise, take your bed and walk" (John 5:8), then later told him, "Sin no more, lest a worse thing come upon you" (5:14). We see Jesus focusing on a change within; He wasn't so concerned about the world around Him. Ruthless leaders crucified Christ, the One who could have called ten thousand angels to set Him free (Matthew 26:53). After Christ left for heaven, those same rulers were left in place to persecute the Christians who were spreading the liberating gospel message.

As the gospel message spread during this persecution period, the church became strong. But as time went on, it began to lose its power. The church became infiltrated with those of a less than pure agenda. It began to have the same desire as that of the Jews—to set up God's kingdom upon this earth.

Such wrong thinking and wrong leadership put the church in a dark place for many years. It became especially bad in the fourth century when Rome's Emperor Constantine united church and state, making the church wander further from its mission. According to the historian Eusebius, Constantine saw the sign of the cross in the sky with the words "In this sign thou shalt conquer"—something that happened immediately before his victory over his rival Maxentius in the year 312 a.d. Wars began to develop to Christianize the world in an attempt to make a kingdom upon this earth.

It was hard to know who was in control during this period—church or state. Those who questioned the church about doctrine or ways of worship were usually accused of heresy and excommunicated, which according to the established church at that time was a sentence to hell. For many years, religious leaders and kings would vie for power over the people, and this contest would result in much blood being shed in the name of Christ. They may have considered this the kingdom of God upon the earth, but in reality it looked more like the kingdom of Satan.

Moving up in history, there were others professing to be Christians who tried to set up their version of a kingdom of God upon this earth with disastrous results. After the Crusades, there was the Spanish Inquisition, then Saint Bartholomew's Day Massacre in France, the pogroms in eastern Europe, and the Holocaust in the Nazi-controlled countries during World War II. It was bad theology leading to bad behavior.

It's an ominous sign when we see Christians departing from the spirit of grace and embracing crusade-like tactics, even to the point of talking about taking up arms to bring about His kingdom on earth. Will the sword advance the kingdom of God? Jesus told Peter, "Put your sword in its place, for all who take the sword will perish by the sword" (Matthew 26:52).

Many today are determined to have a nation or kingdom on this earth with Christian values in family, government, the sciences, the arts, and the media. That would be great, but remember what Jesus said: "The kingdom of God is within you" (Luke 17:21 kjv). He also said, "My kingdom is not of this world. If My kingdom were of this world, My servants would fight, so that I should not be delivered to the Jews; but now My kingdom is not from here" (John 18:36).

Christ's victories are won by spiritual means, not by forcing others to adhere to a set of moral principles. "For the weapons of our warfare are not carnal but mighty in God for pulling down strongholds" (2 Corinthians 10:4). The making of a Christian nation is very appealing, and sometimes this crusader mentality dominates church leadership. The message sent out is this: "Good Christian men, rise up and take control."

Crusades which are evangelistic meetings presenting the gospel are fine, but crusades for forcing our Christian values on the unbelieving heart will never work. Even if successful, the result would only be a nation with forced Christian values, making it impossible to distinguish between those who are the wheat and those who are tares. A so-called Christian nation might be established, and it might make people feel secure being under this Christian umbrella, but it becomes a false sense of security as they mistakenly think they're right with God. With this so-called Christian nation, there would be little contrast between church and state, with everyone thinking they're just a little different shade of gray from their neighbor when it comes to sinfulness. This type of Christian government is just another form of legalism with no saving quality.

Another problem with enforcing our Christian values on the unbelieving heart is that many will draw back from us, because it goes against their nature. It will cause friction and division and alienate ourselves from the very people we're trying to draw to Christ. What we need is to approach them in a loving and meek manner, not hatefully because they aren't believing what we believe.

Even if we were able to convert the world to our moral perspective, that's all it would be—a moral conversion with no internal conversion. Our desire for others should be that they're drawn to God by the Holy Spirit, then convicted of their sin, repent and are forgiven. They should see in us something more than just a higher set of moral principles; they should see a life changed by Him which gives them hope.

The crusaders hated and killed those who didn't think and worship as they did. The gospel should have been presented to the lost in a loving and meek manner, not in a hateful way. We cannot hate people for their moral views, for we were once caught up in that same type of thinking. Any type of resentment we have toward them will reveal itself in the tone of our voice when we speak to them.

Charles Spurgeon expressed it this way:

> For us to hate those who are in error, or talk to
> them with contempt or wish them ill, or do them
> wrong, is not according to the Spirit of Christ. You
> cannot cast out Satan by Satan, nor correct error by
> violence, nor overcome hate by hate. The conquering
> weapon of the Christian is love.

Focus on "Be holy, for I am holy" (1 Peter 1:16), and not on the ungodliness of others. It's easier to try to straighten out others than ourselves; which may be one reason why so many are on a crusade today to straighten out the world. The fact is, when Christ returns again *He* will set up His millennial kingdom upon the earth, and right now it is our hearts that need to change.

Every cause that comes between the Lord and my heart must be cut down. "For the Lord, whose name is Jealous, is a jealous God" (Exodus 34:14). He is "jealous" of the affections we give to something else or another.

Around the year 1400, the Czech theologian John Hus appeared on the scene and preached personal piety and encouraged the masses to use their mind and their God-given right to understand the Bible without being told what to believe. John Hus was preaching some of the key elements for developing a relationship with God, but for the established church at that time, it was still forbidden to question the church's authority and their interpretation of Scripture and of how God should be worshiped. John Hus's effort in trying to change things ended in his being burned at the stake for his radical views.

God later raised up others to continue the reformation of the church. Men like Martin Luther, Ulrich Zwingli, John Calvin, Thomas Crammer, and John Knox took up the torch and set a blaze across the world. They were setting the church back on solid ground

We as Christians need to make sure we're on solid ground today, and haven't strayed from God's purpose for us. We need to use our God-given brain to obey this biblical command: "Study to show thyself approved unto God, a good workman that needeth not be ashamed, rightly dividing the word of truth" (2 Timothy 2:15 kjv). We need to find out for ourselves what the truth is, and not let someone else do the thinking for us.

The church at Ephesus during apostolic times had lost their way; they had lost their "first love," and were told "to repent," or else their lampstand would be taken from them (Revelation 2:15). We cannot afford to lose our "first love" for some cause.

Many of our feelings and strong desires to set up His kingdom on earth are present because we've been conditioned to think that Christian family values are of the utmost importance and should be fought for to protect our rights. This is important for us as Christians, but we cannot rush into this with a crusader-like mentality to force our morals on others. There are peaceful means to influence society rather than militant ones.

Think about what our primary mission is, as seen in this answer from Jesus when He was asked about the greatest commandment in Scripture: "Love the Lord with all your heart, with all your soul, and with all your mind. This is the first commandment. And the second is like it: You shall love your neighbor as yourself" (Matthew 22:37-39). We have enough to do to keep ourselves right with God rather than attempting to make our neighbor change his values. We're to love our neighbors, no matter their beliefs. As long as Satan can keep our eyes and heart set on trying to conform this world to godly principles, and as long as he can concentrate our focus on the sins of others and not our own, he knows he's doing just fine.

It's a natural feeling to be upset in the way society is going, but we need to see how the Lord will use this present world to bring about change. When Christians observe the moral fiber of their country decaying, they're distraught and want to fight to bring things back into order. It's a natural and frustrating experience when living in this type of society, but keep in mind that as the world comes to an end, it's going to get worse and worse (2 Timothy 3:15).

The world is not our home, and we're not here to try to make it our home. Egypt was not the Israelites' home either. When the people of Israel left Egypt, Pharaoh and his army had them pinned against the Red Sea. What did God's people do? They were stuck and had to wholly rely on the Lord for deliverance. That's a good strategy for us as well. We're to rest in God, not in a passive sense but in a praying and believing sense that the Lord will do a great work, just as He initially did when He redeemed us from our old life.

When we're in a crisis, we as humans have a tendency to want to do something about it, but we may be fighting against something we cannot win—like trying to force the world to accept our Christian values. I don't mean we shouldn't use our influence to change things for the better. But we need patience enough to "stand still" and see how the Lord will work.

A. W. Pink comments upon the words of Moses to Israel in Exodus 14:13, "Stand still, and see the salvation of the Lord":

> "Stand still." All attempts at self-help must end. All activities of the flesh must cease. The workings of nature must be subdued. Here is the right attitude of faith in the presence of a trial— "stand still." This is impossible to flesh and blood. All who know, in any measure, the restlessness of the human heart under anticipated trial and difficulty, will be able to form some conception of what is involved in standing still. Nature must be doing something. It will rush hither and thither. It would feign have some hand in the matter. And although it may attempt to justify and sanctify its worthless doings, by bestowing upon them the imposing and popular title of "a legitimate use of means," yet are they the plain and positive fruits of unbelief, which always shut out God, and sees naught save every dark cloud of its own creation. Unbelief creates or magnifies difficulties, and then sets us about removing them by our own bustling and fruitless actions, which, in reality, do but raise a dust around us which prevents our seeing God's salvation.
>
> "Faith, on the contrary, raises the soul above the difficulty, straight to God Himself, and enables one to "stand still." We gain nothing by our restless and

anxious efforts. We cannot make one hair white or black, nor add one cubit to our stature. What could Israel do at the Red Sea! Could they dry it up? Could they level the mountains? Could they annihilate the hosts of Egypt? Impossible! There they were, enclosed within an impenetrable wall of difficulties, in view of which nature could but tremble and feel its own impotency. But this was just the time for God to act. When unbelief is driven from the scene, then God can enter; and in order to get a proper view of His actings, we must 'stand still.' Every movement of nature is, so far as it goes, a positive hindrance to our perception and enjoyment of divine interference on our behalf." (C. H. Mackintosh, *Notes on the Pentateuch*; as quoted in A. W. Pink's *Gleanings in Exodus*)

This tactic of "standing still" puts the control into God's hands. Moses, the leader of the wilderness wanderers, learned to give up control to God, and he was called the meekest and most humble man on all the earth (Numbers 12:3). In his meek position, he was a great leader. Not many leaders today have that quality. "The meek shall inherit the earth" (Matthew 5:5), not the militant. The militant take control; the meek give up control. The meek give up control because they know God is in control.

"Stand still" in your crucified position in Christ, and see what the Lord will do. "Stand still" and remember the oneness we have in Christ: "I am the vine, you are the branches. He who abides in Me, and I in Him, bears much fruit; for without Me you can do *nothing*" (John 15:5). "Stand still" and see how the Lord will change those He has called out of this world. Observe how the Spirit will triumph over the archenemy.

It's of utmost importance to avoid the mistakes of those who made history in a disgraceful sense. Many went wrong because they thought they knew how to set up Christ's kingdom upon this earth. Wasn't that the goal for those so-called Christian slaveholders, and for two-thirds of the Lutheran church during Hitler's time?

A better example for us to follow is the church in Philadelphia, which Jesus commended in these words: "You have a little strength, have kept My word, and have not denied My name" (Revelation 3:8). This church can be compared with the missionary church that saw many revivals in the eighteenth and nineteenth centuries. These are the centuries that gave us such people as George Whitefield, John and Charles Wesley, Jonathan Edwards, Charles Spurgeon, David Livingstone, Hudson Taylor, D. L. Moody, and J. C. Ryle. Besides the spiritual revival that came from this movement, there also came the birth of a great nation, the United States. The Lord put in place leaders who would draft a constitution meant to ensure freedom for all, no matter their religion, race, or other individual differences. It may have been the best attempt in history in upholding the rights of the people and the church, but then again it is only as good as the substance of the people.

Many Christians today in the United States think things have gone very wrong. But it's not the constitution that's the problem, but the moral decay of society. Many have become so frustrated about trying to change things through the democratic system that they find themselves thinking about a forced change of some kind. But before proceeding with civil unrest, they should keep in mind history; keep in mind those Christians in the South who led their states to secede from the Union in order to maintain their right to keep slaves. Then there were those Christians who gave up their democratic government in order to support Hitler, for he presented himself as a champion of Christian values.

But maybe the whole reason for this unrest today among both Christians and non-Christians is a desire for control and power over others. Disguising their motives with good Christian principles furthers their cause, and can be very effective. Let us use this same argument in our view against the morality in China. If we don't like their human and moral stance, should we use military action to change them (which might bring devastation to both countries)? Or should we show by example, prayer, and diplomacy what it is to be a follower of Christ?

God is like an orchestra's conductor, and we His instruments. He desires us to be brought into tune with His suffering Son. He chose to deliver us from ourselves unto Him so we can walk with Him. God says, "See, I have inscribed you on the palms of My hands" (Isaiah 49:16). In other words, our names were written on His hands, those hands that were nailed to the cross to bring us into the great concert with the Father.

Separation from this type of relationship with God is what we should fear most, because this is where we can lose our passion not only for Him but for life itself. The One who resides in us is the One in whom "we live and move and have our being" (Acts 17:28 niv). For everything temporary is just "vanity and vexation of spirit" (Ecclesiastes 1:14 kjv). Christ alone satisfies the heart, and unless we move away from the temporary, we won't be freed from fear, distress, and sorrow. History will prove who we really are—either those with a divided heart and only a surface religion, or a strong church that loved God, having the life of God within and loving others as ourselves.

> Be anxious for nothing, but in everything by prayer and supplication, with thanksgiving, let your requests be made known to God; and the peace of God, which surpasses all understanding, will keep your hearts and minds through Christ Jesus. (Philippians 4:6-7)

This means not being anxious for our country's future, or about worldwide unrest, or about when we'll be translated to heaven, or about the unsaved, or about our own plans and schemes, or about our troubling thoughts—etc., etc. Trust Him, and leave those things in His care. We aren't to be indifferent to what is happening. We're to work as much as we can to make things right, while doing it in as calm a manner as Christ did while He was on this earth.

CHAPTER 23

A PILGRIM'S PATH

A moral change in character, or even a mental change that sees what Christ has brought about in us, is practically useless unless God has made an internal change in our life that passes us from death unto life. This new birth is a miracle of grace, for "you He made alive, who were dead in trespasses and sins" (Ephesians 2:1). A life of faith now lifts us above this world unto another world which is unseen. Our affections are no longer to be set on this world but are fixed on the things of God. In fact, "Friendship with the world is enmity against God" (James 4:4). We should no longer be afraid of what the world brings upon us—the difficulties, the temptations. If our hearts are so concerned with what's going on in the world, the things of heaven will become unreal to us.

For God to deliver us from this world and from our old nature, our acknowledgment of our spiritual bankruptcy is necessary. Unless a miracle of grace is done in our lives, we're like an unkempt garden filled with weeds.

"Blessed are those who mourn: for they shall be comforted" (Matthew 5:4). We're to mourn over our pitiful condition and how we fall short in pleasing God. We ought to see ourselves as He sees us. We ought to mourn over what isn't right in our life, and confess it to God.

Believers mourn in this life, while unbelievers will mourn in the next life. If we continue in sin, we grieve the One who's trying to make us "conformed to the image of His Son" (Ephesians 4:30;

Romans 8:29). God's purpose is not only to forgive us of our sins but to free us from our sinful condition. At present, this is not perfection, but a taste of that perfection. When we confess our sins as believers, we're made clean by the same One who forgave us our sins at regeneration. The cleansing process is just as much a fact as our forgiveness, because "how shall we who died to sin live any longer in it?" (Romans 6:2). Only when a miracle of grace is performed in our hearts can we be conformed into what God wants us to be, "for without Me you can do nothing" (John 15:5).

"For the eyes of the Lord are on the righteous, and His ears are open to their prayers" (1 Peter 3:12). He hears the prayers of the righteous. We can get to where He wants us with a mindset like David's: "Search me, O God, and know my heart: try me, and know my thoughts: and see if there be any wicked way in me, and lead me in the way everlasting" (Psalms 139:23-24 kjv). As the Holy Spirit makes inroads into our life, we're to "rejoice and be glad" (Psalm 118:24), for a great work is being done to make us like Him. If we seem a little out of step with the world, or even persecuted for our beliefs, it is all right. "Blessed are those who are persecuted for righteousness' sake, for theirs is the kingdom of heaven" (Matthew 5:10).

We've been looking at how people in history responded to God's call, some in a good way, some not. When Abraham was going about his business, he had a call from God: "Now the Lord had said to Abram [Abraham]: get out of your country, from your family and your father's house, to a land I will show you" (Genesis 12:1). The new land that Abraham was called to was the land of promise. By faith he left his country and dwelt in this strange land, Canaan. In this place which God had called him to, he possessed no land, nor did he take up with its politics. He was socially distant from its people and did not take part in its religion. Abraham was a "sojourner and pilgrim" in this land at this time. God wanted Abraham for His own, and did not want him engaged with what was going on in the world around him.

As time went on, Abraham's descendants ended up in Egypt and were held there as slaves. After being under Egyptian domination for over four hundred years, God freed the Israelites from their captivity, and they were told to go back to the land of Canaan and conquer it.

As we've seen, the wilderness wanderers—because of their unbelief—failed to get to their land of promise. They did not heed their calling, so they died in the wilderness. Then their descendants—led by Joshua and Caleb—crossed the Jordan River and entered the promised land and conquered it. While conquering this land, they were told by God to drive out the inhabitants living there.

These are all pictures to show God's plan to us. As Christians, in this world we are "sojourners and pilgrims" (1 Peter 2:11), and we're told to drive out sin in our life. We're told, "Reckon yourselves to be dead unto sin, but alive to God in Christ Jesus our Lord. Therefore do not let sin reign in your mortal body, that you should obey it in its lust" (Romans 6:11-12).

For God to achieve His purpose in us, correction and guidance are necessary. "If you are without chastening, of which all have become partakers, then you are illegitimate and not sons" (Hebrews 12:8). Teachers of the Word sometimes over-stress the glorious new life in Christ without telling their hearers about the Lord's chastening of his sons (Hebrews 12:5-7). Then when that chastisement comes, it may disappoint and discourage them because this is not what they expected.

No matter what we're going through, God will encourage us in our journey as pilgrims and sojourners, but it will be necessary for Him to resolve some lingering sin problems in our life. Abraham, Jacob, and David came under the "chastening of the Lord" (Hebrews 12:5) so that they would know the Lord in a more intimate way, with better ability to overcome the world, the flesh, and the devil. We also will face trials, and God uses these trials to show us our inadequacies, our failings, our temperaments, and our desires, so we can flee to His grace.

God's will "will be done on earth as it is in heaven" (Matthew 6:10). This means that we, as God's people, will be cleansed, and we're "predestined to be conformed to the image of His Son" (Romans 8:29). This may take some time, for we're frequently quite stubborn to receive what He wants us to have. But it will be done, for "He who has begun a good work in you will complete it"

(Philippians 1:6), and "He who calls you is faithful, who also will do it" (1 Thessalonians 5:23).

We receive the graces of God because He is pleased to give them to us. For the most part, they're not learned in colleges or seminaries, or given to us because a preacher, teacher, or church bestows them. Rather, they come upon us because we're moving in the direction in which God is directing us.

It isn't until our proud spirit is broken and we're completely surrendered to Him that we're truly growing "in the grace and knowledge of our Lord and Savior Jesus Christ" (2 Peter 3:18). No matter our age, it's a daily process. We take up the yoke He gave us to bear, and then we rest that burden back on His shoulders. "Take My yoke upon you, and learn from Me, for I am gentle and lowly in heart, and you will find rest for your souls" (Matthew 11:29). Nicholas Herman and J. C. Ryle found this rest in their souls when they saw how it was not their work that pleased God, but when they allowed His presence to enter their lives.

But we must be cautious in our walk so as not to be ignorant when an inner voice leads us in a certain direction. The leading may be very appealing, but this appeal may be because of some personal desire in us to go in that direction, or an unfamiliar spirit that wants us led in their direction. We saw examples of individuals and groups who followed the wrong path. We must approach all things that come into our life with knowledge, understanding, and a surety of His written Word. You cannot just awake in the morning with the thought "Where will your Spirit lead me today, Lord?" You must have a rational mindset to filter and check all the thoughts entering your mind. We can be easily misled and look very foolish by following a wrong path.

"Every good gift and every perfect gift is from above, and cometh down from the Father of lights" (James 1:17 kjv). God gave Abraham the power that upheld his soul. Abraham would have sank in utter despair and been engulfed in utter unbelief if God hadn't provided the faith for him to leave his homeland, and then sustained him throughout his life. We need what Abraham had—a faith that believed God's plan, even to the point that if he sacrificed his son Isaac, as God commanded him to do, God would have the power to raise Isaac up from the dead (Hebrews 11:17-19).

We need to let go of our lives to God—not in a reckless way, but in a sober-minded and scriptural way, even though at times we may also not understand. "Trust in the Lord with all your heart, and lean not on your own understanding; in all your ways acknowledge Him, and He shall direct your paths" (Proverbs 3:56). When Abraham finished his journey, God said to him, "Now I know that thou fearest God" (Gen 22:12 kjv). God was satisfied with Abraham, and Abraham had a clear conscience before God. He enjoyed the peace God provided and had a close walk with Him. We need to be on that same pilgrim path, and may God bless us as we journey on. His ultimate purpose for us is to draw us into the story, so we can have a relationship with Him as did Abraham, Isaac, Jacob, Joseph, Moses, and others with their same faith.

It was said of some of the faithful in Old Testament history that they "through faith subdued kingdoms, worked righteousness, obtained promises, stopped the mouths of lions"; they're described as being those "of whom the world was not worthy." (Hebrews 11:33, 38). They were the ones who forsook all and became His disciples. For as Jesus said, "Whoever of you does not forsake all that he has cannot be my disciple" (Luke 14:33). If we hold something back in our life, as Ananias and Sapphira did, then we too will suffer the consequences. "God will not be mocked" (Galatians 6:7); He will not bless those who remain selfish, keeping something for themselves.

For us to be like those of the past who walked with God, we need the faith that God gave them. This faith is the same as its Author. There can be no improvement in this faith; it is God's faith in us. From Scripture we see that our faith has its origin in God: "For by grace are you saved through faith, and that not of yourselves: it is the gift of God, not of works, lest any man should boast" (Ephesians 2:8 kjv). If we were the ones who decided to come to Him, we would have some reason to boast. But we came to Him because an irresistible urge compelled us. We were responsible to believe, but the thought to believe was given to us by God.

Then after our believing, a post-salvation faith comes that realizes: "I am crucified with Christ: nevertheless I live, yet not

I, but Christ liveth in me: and the life which I now live in the flesh I live by the *faith of the Son of God,* who loved me, and gave himself for me (Galatians 2:20 kjv). He who walks in this faith, walks freely and clearly, and he isn't discouraged by circumstances, the criticisms of men, or the way the world is heading.

It's not only our faith that has its origin in God; *any* good in us is from God. "For He made Him who knew no sin to be sin for us, that we might become the righteousness of God in Him" (2 Corinthians 5:21). There dwells in us now not only the faith of God but the righteousness of God as well. Our sin was imputed or given to Christ, and His righteousness is imputed or given to us. This is a theological fact that should be experienced.

"He who did not spare His own Son, but delivered Him up for us all, how shall He not with Him also freely give us *all* things?" (Romans 8:32). We cannot fathom what a sacrifice it was for God to have His Son go through what He did—the humiliation, the suffering, and most of all the bearing of our sins. God did this so that we might obtain "all things." Believe this. Rest on this fact, and move forward in your journey.

When we have that in mind, "Who shall separate us from the love of Christ? Shall tribulation, or distress, or persecution, or famine, or nakedness, or peril, or sword?" (Romans 8:35). No, nothing shall separate us from the love of Christ, for we are "more than conquerors through Him who loves us" (Romans 8:37), and we have the "boldness to enter the Holies by the blood of Jesus, by a new and living way which He consecrated for us" (Hebrews 10:19).

"If the Spirit of Him who raised Jesus from the dead dwells in you, He who raised Christ from the dead will also give life to your mortal bodies through His Spirit who dwells in you" (Romans 8:11). This same Spirit who raised Jesus from the dead now resides in us, and He will bring us from death unto life. This Spirit is not a mere influence, but a person—God in us.

Personally speaking, there was a time after I first came to Christ—or rather, when He first came to me—when I felt somewhat uncomfortable with myself. I knew the burden of guilt had been lifted from me, but as time went on, I became uneasy with myself, knowing how truly sinful I still was and how far short I fell in pleasing the Lord. I was realizing that the fruit of my labors to please God was what the Bible called "fruit after its own kind" (Genesis 1:24-25), unlike the fruit of the Holy Spirit "after its kind."

Although I knew that other believers apparently sinned as much as I did, I couldn't get away from thinking that I was the worst sinner I knew. I realized my spiritual bankruptcy, and I mourned and humbled myself before God.

As I contemplated my condition, I realized the Holy Spirit had entered into me (1 Corinthians 3:16), and I truly was the temple of God (1 Corinthians 3:16). Whatever good fruits my life would bear would have to originate from the One residing in me. I could say with Paul, "In me (that is, in my flesh) dwelleth no good thing" (Romans 7:18 kjv). The "love, joy, peace, longsuffering, gentleness, goodness, faith, meekness, temperance" (Galatians 5:22-23 kjv) was not to be worked for or prayed for, because it was already given me at the time of my salvation. I needed to be aware of any sin creeping into my life that I hadn't owned up to, repented of, and given over to God to get control over. When I became honest with God about my true condition, I gave room in my life for God to work, and a mighty work it has been.

Let's return again to the wisdom of Solomon, who after looking at the vanity of life said this: "The conclusion of the whole matter: Fear God and keep His commandments, for this is man's all" (Ecclesiastes 12:13). Any other life becomes misleading. With a healthy fear of the Lord, we're to "be anxious for nothing, but in everything by prayer and supplication, with thanksgiving, let your requests be known to God; and the peace of God, which surpasses all understanding, will guard your hearts and minds through Christ Jesus" (Philippians 4:6-7). By being fervent in prayer and thanksgiving, we allow God to orchestrate the affairs of the world and the direction of our life.

We end this book with the story of John Newton. Born in London on July 24, 1725, he went to sea at an early age and became involved in the slave trade. While at sea, during a violent storm in which he thought he might die, he asked the Lord for mercy. He began to study the Bible diligently and to understand more of what God's mercy and grace was all about. He went on to become a minister of the Word and a campaigner for abolishing the practice of slavery in England. To make his messages more affective, he put some of his content into lyrical form. One result was the song "Amazing Grace."

Although Newton was the author of the lyrics for "Amazing Grace," he had no tune for it. The people sang or chanted this to whatever tune they wanted. Then around 1835, an American Baptist song leader and compiler of tunes named William Walker set "Amazing Grace" to the melody we're so familiar with today. The source of this melody is unknown, but may well have come from the Afro-American culture, since Walker lived in the southern part of the United States. It's a soulful melody, much like other soulful songs sung by Afro-American slaves.

Then there's that last verse of "Amazing Grace," starting with the line "When we've been there ten thousand years"—a verse that John Newton did not write, but which came later. This verse was sung many years in Afro-American worship before it appears at the conclusion of "Amazing Grace" as published by Edwin Othello Excell in 1910.

"Amazing Grace" was developed because John Newton contemplated the atrocities he'd committed and the amazing grace of God to forgive Him for what he'd done. Why the Afro-Americans had to go through such suffering is perplexing. But for us to keep from feeling so overwhelmed with what has happened in the past or with what is happening now, let's keep in mind the words of Isaiah:

"For My thoughts are not your thoughts,
nor are your ways My ways," says the Lord.
"For as the heavens are higher than the earth,
So are My ways higher than your ways,
And My thoughts than your thoughts." (Isaiah 55:89)

In *Thoughts upon the African Slave Trade*, John Newton wrote, "I hope it will always be a subject of humiliating reflection to me that I was once an active instrument in a business at which my heart now shudders." We've all messed up in life, and we've all taken part in injustices in some way or other, even if only sins of omission (such as not helping those in need) versus the sins of commission (which are sins we actively commit). To experience the inexhaustible grace of God in the saving of our soul, and then to experience His love, joy, peace, longsuffering, kindness, goodness, faithfulness, gentleness, self-control, is what our soul desires, and we won't be satisfied until we have it.

After experiencing such grace, we should experience the truths of Isaac Newton's hymn flowing naturally from our heart, soul, mind, and mouth:

> Amazing grace, how sweet the sound
> that saved a wretch like me!
> I once was lost, but now am found,
> was blind, but now I see.
>
> 'Twas grace that taught my heart to fear
> and grace my fears relieved;
> how precious did that grace appear
> the hour I first believed!
>
> Through many dangers, toils, and snares
> I have already come;
> 'tis grace that brought me safe thus far,
> and grace will lead me home.
>
> The Lord has promised good to me,
> His word my hope secures;
> He will my shield and portion be
> as long as life endures.
>
> When we've been there ten thousand years,
> bright shining as the sun,
> we've no less days to sing God's praise
> than when we first begun.

Imitating and thinking like Christ can bring us only so far; but having His mind and life in us allows something far greater to happen. Having experienced this, we can look back and realize how far we've already come. We first believed because of the strong conviction of sin that came upon us. As time went on, we may have felt guilty about how far short we've come in pleasing Him, but after a complete surrender of our will, the struggle and effort ceases. With a new singleness of purpose, we moved away from the intellectual approach of our faith to the spiritual rest and confidence we were meant to have.

Only as we continue on this journey of exalting and drawing upon Him do we blossom. As His life-giving water flows through us, there should be little anxiety from whatever dangers, toils, and snares we encounter, for we are where He wants us—in this mysterious union with Him by grace.

Printed in the United States
by Baker & Taylor Publisher Services

Printed in the United States
by Baker & Taylor Publisher Services